# Spanish Flu and Covid-19 in Western Europe: The Basque Case

Basque politics series, No. 19

# Spanish Flu and Covid-19 in Western Europe: The Basque Case

Anton Erkoreka

Center for Basque Studies
University of Nevada, Reno
2021

This book was published with generous financial support from the Government of Bizkaia.

Center for Basque Studies
University of Nevada, Reno
1664 North Virginia St,
Reno, Nevada 89557 usa
http://basque.unr.edu


ISBN-13: 978-1-949805-56-7


English translation and adaptation for English-speaking readers by Eider Etxebarria Zuluaga.
Cover Design by Rebecca Lown

Library of Congress Cataloging-in-Publication Data

Names: Erkoreka, Anton, author.
Title: Spanish flu and COVID-19 in Western Europe and the Basque country /
Anton Erkoreka.
Description: [Reno?] : [Center for Basque Studies Press?], 2021. | Series:
Basque politics series ; 19 | Includes bibliographical references.
Identifiers: LCCN 2021025526 | ISBN 9781949805567 (paperback)
Subjects: LCSH: Influenza--History--20th century. | Epidemics--History. |
Spanish flu. | COVID-19 (Disease)
Classification: LCC RA644.I6 E753 2021 | DDC 614.5/18--dc23
LC record available at https://lccn.loc.gov/2021025526

# Contents

"And the flood was forty days upon the earth; and the waters increased, and bare up the ark. . . . And all flesh died that moved upon the earth, both birds, and cattle, and beasts, and every creeping thing that creepeth upon the earth, and every man: all in whose nostrils was the breath of the spirit of life, of all that was on the dry land, died. . . .

And the waters prevailed upon the earth a hundred and fifty days. . . . God made a wind to pass over the earth, and the waters assuaged. . . . And the ark rested in the seventh month, on the seventeenth day of the month, upon the mountains of Ararat . . . the tops of the mountains seen. And it came to pass at the end of forty days, that Noah opened the window of the ark which he had made. . . . And God spake unto Noah, saying, Go forth from the ark . . . be fruitful, and multiply upon the earth."

(Genesis 7.17–8.17)

# Acknowledgements

Thank you to all the archivists and librarians who have kindly taken care of me and helped me over these years. Thanks to Aitor Erkoreka for his invaluable help in the design of templates and drawing up the graphics; Mikel Erkoreka for proofing the manuscript and his collaboration; Nieves Gonzáles and Leire Erkoreka for their support; Aitor Anduaga and Begoña Madarieta of the Basque Museum of Medical History; Josu Hernando of the same museum and the *Grupo de Investigación de Demografía Histórica e Historia Urbana (UPV/EHU)*; Michel Duvert and Pierre Thillaud for their invaluable help in the Northern Basque Country; David Mariezkurrena for his help in Navarre; Ander Manterola, Gurutzi Arregi, and other members of the Etniker ethnographic research groups which are working on the *Atlas Etnográfico de Vasconia*, the great project of our teacher, Jose Miguel de Barandiaran; and also Joan March, of the *Grup d'Investigació d'Història de la Salut (Universitat de les Illes Balears)*, for sharing initiatives and research during the 2020 pandemic.

Finally, I would like to thank senior university students on my "Society, Science and Technology" at the *Aulas de la Experiencia* (UPV/EHU) because they have intellectually enriched me. Also, to my young university students, in the first and third years of their medicine degrees (UPV/EHU), who have collaborated, throughout several academic years, by collecting data from ecclesiastical and civil archives of various locations around the Basque Country, for their internships on my subjects of *Historia de la medicina y documentación médica* and *Euskal medikuntzaren historia*. Some people have told me that this first contact with the history of pandemics in their hometowns has provided them with an enriching experience, which will probably be useful to them during the important work they are now carrying out as doctors during the COVID-19 pandemic that began in 2020. My apologies if I forget to name anybody who investigated the towns I mention in this book. Abarrategi, A.; Arocena, M.; Aiestaran, K.; Aizpurua, I.; Aldazabal, M.; Alberdi, I.; Aramburu, A.; Aranberri, A.; Aranzeta, J.; Arbelaitz, N.; Areitio, L.; Arratibel, N.; Arrizabalaga, I.; Artola, K.; Arzelus, M.; Atutxa, L.; Azaldegi, G.; Azkune, O.; Azkune, I.; Barceló, I.; Bárcena, N.; Bhati Azkoaga, K.; Brouard, I.; Camera, A.; Quarry, S.; Capetillo, N.; Lawns, K.; Cibrian, F.; Crespo, A.M.; Emaldi, A.; Errasti, A.; Etxart, E.; Fernandez Rived, I.; Gabilondo, A.; Ganzarain, M.; Garcia Lombardía, K.; Garcia Ulazia, G.; Gómez Suarez, N.; Gurrutxaga, A.; Hidalgo, G.; Hinojal, B.; Iceta, U.; Ingelmo, N.; Intxausti, T.; Izusta, M.; Larrea, A.; Laserna, B.; Legaristi, N.; López Gutierrez, M.; Madariaga, A.; Madarieta, B.; Maqueda, A.; Martin, J.C.; Niso, J.J.; Ocerin, I.; Odriozola, I.; Otegi, I.; Otegi, N.; Pigeon, N.; Palazuelos, I.; Perez de Nanclares, M.; Pipaon, J.; Ramajo, O.;

Round, E.; Retolaza, S.; Saavedra, I.; Sagasta, A.; Santiago, S.; Urizarbarrena, I.; Valero, L.; Zabala, S.; and Zubimendi, O.

# Introduction

The word *pandemic* is defined in the dictionary as an "epidemic disease that extends to many countries," although its practical scope is much broader than that. A pandemic is not only the consequence of a microorganism that extends to many countries: to that we must add its contagion and mortality rates; its side effects and aftermaths for the infected; its demographic, economic, political, and social repercussions; and its impact on education, habits, and public and private aspects of life. All of this is why, when we talk about the Spanish flu and COVID-19 pandemics, caused by two viruses known as influenza (H1N1) and SARS-CoV-2, respectively, we are referring to a whole set of factors and circumstances that must be taken into account. To understand this, one only has to take into account the way that science fiction literature and films portray large pandemics and major wars as the origins of future apocalyptic worlds, and new social orders.[1]

Examining the history of diseases and analyzing emerging and re-emerging pathologies that have taken center stage over the last forty years (along with cancer, AIDS, Ebola, etc.), it was often thought and written that some great pandemic was bound to take place at the beginning of the

1 "Liberalism, needless to say, died of anthrax." Huxley, Aldous. *Un mundo feliz (Brave New World).* Mexico, Editores Mexicanos Unidos, 2017. p. 45.

twenty-first century.[2] But the general thought was that it was going to be some strain of the influenza virus, or a new virus, which would emerge from the heart of Africa or Asia. It was not anticipated that the main player would be a coronavirus, despite the warnings we received in 2003 and 2012, and the "atypical pneumonia" that appeared in Wuhan in early January 2020, in fact, caught us by surprise. As it spread—first through China, then across Europe, America, and the rest of the world—it was seen to have clear similarities to the first wave of the Spanish flu. There were some notable exceptions, however, such as the age of the deceased, the mortality rate, and the clinical cases' complications and consequences.

Some of the reports and records made by civilian and military doctors—which are kept, for example, in the *Archives du services de santé des armées* (ASSA, French Armed Forces Health Service Archives) and are the most complete sources of information about health during World War I—had always seemed disproportionate, exaggerated, and difficult to interpret, and had been called into question. I would never have anticipated what I have seen while following the development of the 2020 pandemic, and I have begun to better understand the information from 1918, ceasing to doubt its veracity. The new viruses responsible for both pandemics, their process of expansion

---

2 Erkoreka, A. "La gripe española 90 años después" (Spanish flu, 90 years later). *El País,* December 13, 2008 (print edition. Health Supplement). *El País*, May 8, 2009 (digital edition). http://sociedad.elpais.com/sociedad/2009/05/08/actualidad/1241733603_850215.html

around the world, and their consequences, have undoubted parallels.

Those parallels were the impetus behind this book, which aims to offer a rigorous synthesis of the Spanish influenza pandemic, providing novel, original data collected from military, civil, and religious archives. This book's narrative concludes in the summer of 2020, when the second COVID-19 wave began, and therefore also includes a synthesis of the first wave of the current pandemic.

The geographical area I concentrate on are two of the major states in Western Europe: France and Spain. Therefore, I have focused on the Basque Country because I consider it to be a highly significant sample which can be extrapolated to other territories. Spain gave its name to the 1918 flu pandemic because the first wave became visible, and was very intense, in Madrid during May and June of that year. Additionally, having been a neutral country during World War I, Spain's media had more freedom of information.

My research centers on the following four major cities (year studied and corresponding population at the time in parentheses): Paris (1919, 2,906,472); Rome (1920, 651,625); Madrid (1918, 648,760); and Bilbao (1918, 103,172). In 1920, Spain had 20,880,000 inhabitants, and France had 32,830,000. The Basque Country in 1920 had 1,272,645 inhabitants. The Basque Country is divided, in Spain, into two administrative entities: the Basque Autonomous Community, and the Foral Community of Navarre. In France, the three Basque territories are part an administrative community—

The Basque Country Collective Community (Euskal Hirigune Elkargoa in Basque, Communauté d'agglomeration Pays basque in French)—which is part of the département des Pyrénées-Atlantiques.

It should be noted that France was the epicenter of the Great War with which this pandemic is so closely connected. At the time of the Spanish flu, World War I was taking place, and one of its main fronts was in northern France and Belgium. Morrow (2004, 615) estimates that the death toll from the war—almost all the dead being soldiers of different nationalities—was 9.3 million, although other sources raise that figure to 11 million.

## Banalization of the Account of the Spanish Flu Pandemic

A famous doctor from the first half of the nineteenth century, Broussais (1772–1838), called in his time "le Napoléon du Val de Grâce," made a sarcastic comment about flu, considering the disease to be inconsistent and not of major importance. According to his definition, "*Grippe, invention des gens sans le sou et des médecins sans clients qui, n'ayant rien de mieux à faire, ont inventé ce farfadet*" (Flu has been invented by people without money and doctors without clients who, having nothing better to do, have invented this nonsense.)

In the 1830s, there was a very serious cholera pandemic which affected Europe for the first time, and, at the same time, there were two flu pandemics. In the minutes of the Parisian *Academie de Médecine* there are several contributions and discussions about flu and its categorization as a defined illness. Over the following decades, flu was, to an extent, forgotten about, disappearing as a major medical concern until the Russian flu pandemic (1889–1890), which caused major social alarm. Doctors at the time did not distinguish the pandemic from seasonal flus, and over the next several years, when flu appeared, it scared people at first, but being so benign, they ended up paying little attention to it. On some of the bulletins with health statistics from that time, it is not even mentioned. The Spanish flu is what led to its being considered a serious illness once more, but throughout the twentieth century, and to this day, non-specialists still see flu as being relatively benign.

The Spanish flu pandemic took place at the end of World War I. In official accounts of the war and of the pandemic, the latter was overshadowed by the war and post-war political, social, and economic events. Moreover, censorship and war propaganda profoundly altered the perception of what had happened, despite the pandemic having caused four times more deaths than the war. This manipulation of the pandemic is also connected with the circumstances of the cruel carnage of World War I and the inhumane treatment of soldiers at the front. Photos of field hospitals with perfectly ordered beds, and doctors and nurses carefully looking after soldiers sick with Spanish flu, are pure propaganda.

Most of the more than 50,000 American soldiers and hundreds of thousands of soldiers of other nationalities who died of flu, or of its respiratory complications, did so in distressing conditions in the holds of the ships that transported them to Europe, in barracks, or in trenches. The same photographs that the American authorities distributed to the media in the autumn of 1918—to make parents, wives, or children believe that their relatives were well cared for by the army—are still used by the media in 2020. Even today, journalistic features on the Spanish flu include some of those overused propaganda photos, even though some of us, when interviewed on the subject, ask the media not to follow that game now, a hundred years later, and not to use those images. Some advertising and propaganda campaigns, it seems, make their mark, and continue to hypnotize journalists and readers.

The account of the 1918–1920 flu pandemic has been highly manipulated since its origin to the present day. Its cultural connotations were carefully examined by Davis (2013). In May 1918, the Spanish press either belittled or dismissed the flu epidemic, giving it names such as the "Soldier of Naples," the "Fashionable Disease," or, later, the "Spanish Lady," among other things. Some political connotations persist, for instance describing it as the "incorrectly named Spanish flu," which focuses on the insulting nature of the name instead of the real story. Its name should not upset anyone; there is a reason for it. The outbreak in Madrid in the spring of 1918 was very serious and, furthermore, could be reported on with relative freedom (A. Erkoreka 2017). Geographical names that have been used since the nineteenth century (Russian, Italian, Hong Kong...) are not an insult to any country, and are more easily used references to these pandemics than are the years in which they took place. This way of naming pandemics only ceased to be used in the 2009 pandemic because of the Mexican authorities' objection to the name "Mexican flu."

Lobbying from the pork industry also tried to prevent the spread of the term "swine flu," although it failed to do so, and the term is widely used in English-language literature. The name "influenza A (H1N1)" does not seem very appropriate because influenza A has different subtypes, and some of them will probably cause new pandemics or epidemics again in the future. Something similar is true for the "Wuhan pandemic," the "Wuhan coronavirus," or the "Chinese pandemic," terms that the media began using in January and February 2020, and which the Chinese authorities have managed to weaken, distancing China from the coronavirus pandemic in the media and in the public psyche. The pandemic has ended up with the neutral, aseptic term, "COVID-19," China emerging unscathed in every way. There are many of us, however, who think that this pandemic arose, without a doubt, in China—like many other pandemics throughout history.

The conflicting figures about the Spanish flu published in some historical medical articles, especially local ones, are due to the fact that they use different references, different time periods, and/or false or simple sources and data. This is why the results obtained by comparing calculations are sometimes unreliable. The most serious falsehood still circulating today, in 2020, is the claim that 100 million people, or absurd ranges such as "50 to 100 million people," died, both of which leave readers dumbfounded and essentially uninformed about the subject or its seriousness. All of this is despite the hundreds of articles that have been published in the last twenty years and which, by now, have clarified each and every aspect of the pandemic. The huge number of quality papers published (see PubMed) has come to be described by Phillips (2014) as the "recent wave of historiography on Spanish flu," comparing it to the waves of the pandemic itself. Regarding the aforementioned death figures and the manipulation of historical data, I have to say that the 2009 swine influenza pandemic makes us reflect on our current situation because the World Health Organization (WHO) took Spanish flu as a reference then, and false figures of 100 million dead led to an overcalculation of packs of Tamiflu and vaccines—which different states bought to the undoubted profit of several pharmaceutical companies.

I will, therefore, avoid the clichés, anecdotes, manipulations, lies, and mistakes (which unfortunately continue to be repeated systematically, especially on social media). A worldwide pandemic should not be trivialized and downplayed; rather, it deserves a serious and scientific examination.

## Combats pour l'histoire

I have been trying for a few years now to dismantle clichés and manipulations about the 1918–1920 flu pandemic, systematically returning to the original documents from the French Armed Forces Health Services and the American military contingent in Europe during World War I, as well as to the civil and religious records of the time. Regarding this, I would like to recall the French historian Lucien Febvre (1878–1956), co-founder with Marc Bloch of the academic journal *Annales d'histoire* économique *et social*, in 1929. Febvre developed what he called a *histoire-problème*, which is closely linked with the present. Historical facts, he argued, must be described, but, above all, must be explained using all disciplines—medicine, epidemiology, sociology, ethnography, geography, politics, etc. The same is true for the study of the Spanish flu pandemic and the entire range of pandemics over the last 130 years: all resources must be used. Indeed, this is what researchers have been doing over the last twenty years—unearthing corpses in the Alaskan permafrost, investigating anatomical pathology studies carried out by museums on the cadavers of soldiers who died in the Great War and which are held in military institutes, poring over the most implausible archives and documents from all around the world, and collecting the testimonies of survivors and their descendants, and conducting the most advanced genetic studies to examine the evolution of the virus.

As Febvre says very clearly and poetically, in a compilation of articles with the significant title of *Combats pour la l'histoire* (1952, Spanish edition 1986, p. 232), and in another of his works written ten years later:

> Undoubtedly, history is put together using written documents. But it can also be put together, it must be put together, without using written documents if such do not exist. With everything the historian's ingenuity can allow him or her to use. . . . Therefore, in words. With signs. With landscapes and tiles. With field shapes and weeds. With moon eclipses and oxen collars. With expert examinations of stones carried out by geologists, and the analysis of metal swords carried out by chemists. In short: with everything that being a human being depends on; the presence, activity, tastes, and way of being of human beings.

Anton Erkoreka

# Chapter 1
# A Historical Overview

The main culprits of the 1918–1920 influenza pandemic and the coronavirus pandemic that began in 2020, are two viruses that belong to different families but that cause similar clinical cases. Both appeared abruptly and unexpectedly, in 1918 and 2020, respectively, spread from person to person easily by air, and caused very serious pneumonic cases with grave consequences for other organs and systems.

The excess mortality rates they caused in their first waves were practically identical. For example, in Bilbao between May and July 1918, the first few months of the Spanish flu, 0.6 per 1,000 inhabitants died from flu and its respiratory complications. In the Basque Autonomous Community, deaths from COVID-19 between March and June 2020, were between 0.6 and 0.7 per 1,000 inhabitants.

## Influenza A/H1N1

From the year 1500 to the present day, influenza epidemics and pandemics have been documented, and they have occurred repeatedly in a systematic way over the centuries. One of the first accurate descriptions of an epidemic is from 1550, one which caused the death of five percent of the population of England (Wrigley and Schofield, 1981, 336–337).

In medical books from the sixteenth and seventeenth centuries, influenza has been variously referred to as *catarrhus epidemicus, tussis epidemicus*, and *febris catarrhalis epidemica.* There are excellent descriptions of the disease, such as that given by the famous British physician Thomas Sydenham (1624–1689), who devoted a chapter of his work *Opera Medica* to the outbreak of "epidemic coughs" that took place in 1675. In the eighteenth century, in the wake of the flu epidemic of 1780, French author, M. Saillant, published the first monograph on this subject with the significant title *Epidemies catharrales, vulgairement dites la grippe* (Catarrhal epidemics, commonly called the flu).

Since the mid-eighteenth century, the French have called this respiratory illness *grippe* (meaning "claw" or "hook," because the disease "grabs" and has very acute symptoms), and the Italians, and then the English, have called it *influenza* (from Latin and meaning "influence," because it was thought to be linked to external factors such as air, temperature, stars, or miasmas).

At the end of the nineteenth century, Pflüger identified a bacillus in patients' exudates, which he considered to be responsible for the clinical cases, calling it *Haemophilus influenzae.* Today we know that this illness is a virus, and that the bacterium present only produces additional infections. The first human flu virus was discovered in 1933, and was designated with the letter *A*. In 1940, *B* virus was discovered, and *C* virus was identified in 1947. The designation of these genera is based on their antigenic characteristics. Influenza A viruses are subclassified based on hemagglutinin (H) and neuraminidase (N) antigens. Influenza A virus has fifteen H subtypes and nine N subtypes, of which only subtypes H1, H2, H3, N1, and N2 have been linked to diseases affecting people. Specifically, the virus responsible for both the 1918 and 2009 pandemics was H1N1.

Today we understand the antigenic characteristics of the A/H1N1 virus that made it so virulent (Taubenberger et al. 2005; Tumpey et al. 2005), its evolution (Nelson et al. 2008; Smith et al. 2009; Crosby 2003), its persistent legacy (Morens et al. 2009), and a series of external factors that were linked to the Great War whose combination turned out to be explosive. Its preference for young adults was specific to the Spanish flu pandemic that peaked, almost simultaneously around the world, between October and November of 1918.

There are two clinical variants of the flu: one is "seasonal influenza," which appears systematically in the cold months of the year, with clinical cases that, in most of the population, weaken after a week of treatment. For older people and people with other pathologies, this may lead to serious problems and even significant mortality that, in certain years in which the strains are especially virulent, can cause up to half a million deaths worldwide. Several subtypes circulate during each of these seasonal epidemics, the proportion of which varies over the months of the epidemic. During winter in the Northern Hemisphere, they circulate around the hemisphere, but when summer comes, they only circulate in the Southern Hemisphere, during that part of the world's winter. Vaccines used in autumn vaccination campaigns use the influenza subtypes that have circulated in the other hemisphere during the spring, and target risk groups. In addition, several strains are present during each epidemic and, as the epidemic evolves, they change, so that those that predominated at first, move to the background by the end (figure 1.1).

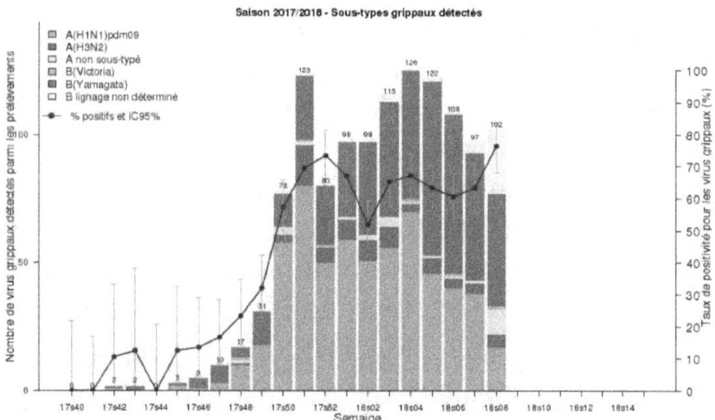


**Prélèvements positifs et taux de positivité** pour les virus grippaux des cas de syndromes grippaux prélevés par les médecins Sentinelles (pédiatres et généralistes) depuis la semaine 2017s40**

Figure 1.1. Influenza subtypes detected in France in the 2017–2018 seasonal epidemic, which was mostly subtype A/H1N1 at first and, by the end of the epidemic, subtype B/Yamagata. Source: *Sentinelles*.

The other variant is "pandemic flu," which appears every twenty to twenty-five years, affecting millions of people worldwide and with very high mortality. For instance, the Spanish flu pandemic of 1918–1920 killed 2.2% of the entire world population.

## SARS-CoV-2

The culprit for the 2020 pandemic is a virus called SARS-CoV-2, which is part of the coronavirus family. The name comes from the crown-shaped bumps on the virus's surface when examined with an electron microscope. The coronavirus family (*Coronaviridae*) was named as such by the International Committee on Taxonomy of Viruses (ICTV) in 1975, with four genera being defined: alpha and beta affecting mammals, and gamma and delta affecting birds. Its origin and main reservoir are bats (Cui 2019; Gozlan 2020).

In the 1930s and 1940s, when coronaviruses began to be identified, they were only considered to be the causes behind zoonoses. Since the 1960s, four of them—HCoV-NL63, HCoV-229E, HCoV-OC43 and HCoV-HKU1—have been seen to be endemic and produce ten to thirty percent of human respiratory infections. They mainly affect children, with mild cases such as colds. This is very important today because some researchers believe that these viruses can create cross-immunity that benefits children, young people, and adults who suffer from these mild cases.[3] Some researchers connect the fact that children and young people have hardly been affected by COVID-19 to this (March and Erkoreka 2020).

The surprise was in 2003 when SARS (Severe Acute Respiratory Syndrome)—produced by a coronavirus identified as SARS-CoV—broke out and affected twenty-nine countries and 8,096 identified patients (774 of whom died). In 2012, a second coronavirus—MERS-CoV—broke out in the Middle East, affecting twenty-eight countries and causing 2,494 cases and 858 deaths. The high degree of lethality of both (9.6% and 34.4% of those affected, respectively) worried health authorities, but nobody expected a new coronavirus that was to spread much more easily than the previous ones, albeit with a lower mortality rate.

And so, it was in November 2019 that the seventh known coronavirus with the capacity to infect humans began circulating in Wuhan (although the Chinese authorities only declared it to the WHO on the last day of the year) and it was given the name COVID-19. On January 9, 2020, it was made public that a pneumonia of unknown origin had broken out in China,[4] and the Chinese authorities then announced that they had isolated the genetic sequence of the new virus.[5] This

---

3 "Coronavirus : une partie de la population pourrait être déjà protégée par une immunité croisée," *Le Monde*, June 4, 2020.

4 "Une pneumonie d'origine inconnue en Chine," *Le Monde*, January 9, 2020.

5 "Un virus similar al SARS, responsable de la misteriosa neumonía china," *El País*, January 11, 2020.

new microorganism, identified as SARS-CoV-2, is responsible for COVID-19, a benign disease in eighty percent of cases, but highly symptomatic in fifteen percent of patients and very serious in five percent.[6]

## Climate, Environment, and Health

The coronavirus crisis obliges us to investigate its origins and the circumstances around it. One of the major factors is the climate change caused by overpopulation, pollution, and mass urbanization—essentially the occupation and mistreatment of our natural environment and ecosystems. Climate change, which we have clearly seen in the twenty-first century, may have led to a virus which had previously only affected bats and has now reached humans. The virus originated in Wuhan, a city that in recent years has grown excessively and has destroyed its entire natural environment, thus having an effect on its flora and fauna. This COVID-19 pandemic, originally, was nothing more than a zoonosis like other emerging diseases such as Ebola, AIDS, and MERS.[7]

The history of the earth's climate (Uriarte 2009) and the effect of climate on human history are of increasing importance (Le Roy 2017), although sometimes not enough emphasis is put on climate's

6 "Coronavirus : au coeur de la bataille immunitaire contre le virus," *Le Monde*, June 12, 2020.

7 Joan March and Anton Erkoreka, "Pandemias, medio ambiente y clima," *Ultima Hora (Palma)*, May 27, 2020.

effect on human health. We must say, without equivocation, that throughout history, climate and environmental imbalances have led to brutal pandemics. I will give three examples of this.

The first cholera pandemic began after the eruption of the volcano Tambora, on Sumbawa Island, to the east of Java, Indonesia, in 1815. Sulfurous aerosols shot up into the air, reaching the stratosphere, and remained there for several years, and that caused widespread cooling which was responsible for what was called the "year without summer" that followed the eruption. That exceptional climate event led to very poor harvests in many parts of the world the following year, and especially in South Asia, leading to famine and major population movements on the Indian subcontinent. In this way, a local disease in the Bengal Delta began to spread. In the first pandemic (1817–1823), it spread throughout Southeast Asia. In the second one (1827–1834), it travelled throughout Asia, Europe, and America, causing enormous mortality and damage. Then came the third (1839–1859), the fourth (1863–1874), and the fifth cholera pandemics (1881–1896), all of which affected the entire nineteenth century.

The Black Plague of 1348 broke out at the onset of what has been called the Little Ice Age, which caused a significant drop in temperature, poor harvests, famines, and changes in the environment and in the distribution of certain disease-transmitting animals such as rodents. A rodent epizootic in central and north Asia was transformed into a pandemic that killed between twenty-five and thirty-three million people in Europe. The Kingdom of Navarre, according to Monteano (2002), had a population of 250,000 people before the plague pandemic, and after it, that figure had fallen to 125,000; in other words, it killed fifty percent of the population. In some towns the figure was even higher; in Lizarra-Estella, for instance, sixty percent of the inhabitants died. In Europe there were almost twenty more plague epidemics over the following four centuries, the last of them taking place in 1720.

The Plague of Justinian, *pestis justinianea*, which took place during the reign of Justinian (527–565) is documented in Ethiopia in 540, in Egypt in 541, and it arrived in Constantinople in May 542, causing the death of 300,000 people. It spread throughout all Mediterranean countries until its end in 544. Presumably, this pandemic—which also affected China and India—started in the terrible year of 536. Some people believe that there was a volcanic eruption in Indonesia or Japan of the same intensity as Tambora, and others that a large meteorite hit the earth. The result was another year without summer, without crops, with famines and environmental imbalances culminating in the Plague of Justinian. We found a very interesting testimony about this in Aquitaine, given by Grégoire de Tours (2012, 135–139) during the reign of Childebert I (King of Paris and Orleans, from 511 to 558). Torrential rain caused major flooding in the Loire and the Rhone valleys. A large fireball swept through the sky producing a great noise. In Bordeaux, the earth tremor forced the population to abandon the city. In the Pyrenees, immense rocks fell and crushed people and cattle to death. Villages and crops were burned down in Bordeaux and Orleans. A great illness followed, for instance a dysentery that spread through Gaul: "*une espèce de dysenterie se répandit dans presque toute la Gaule.*" The epidemic killed many people, including the king's young children and several members of the royal family, such as Queen Austrégilde who, on her deathbed, and in vengeance against the two doctors who had been unable to cure her, asked for them to be killed, which they were.[8]

These three examples serve to illustrate the importance of environmental and climate factors with regard to human health. All three cases are natural phenomena or climate cycles that are not dependent on people; however, in the current climate change process, the responsibility indeed lies with humans.

## Pandemics in Western Europe

During the last millennium, the undoubted main player was the plague that dominated Europe from the fourteenth to the eighteenth century. After its abrupt disappearance in 1720, one of the main causes of death for decades was smallpox, which was reduced by variolation, the antecedent

8 https://www.youtube.com/watch?v=mRZ1_eU8vps

of modern vaccines. At the end of the nineteenth century, the history of medicine was marked by the continuous cholera pandemics that ravaged Europe and the world, and by the endemic tuberculosis that affected large industrial centers above all.

### *1729–2009 Influenza Pandemics*

Among viral pandemics, the seasonal, benign flu breaks out almost every winter; and pandemic flu, sometimes of considerable virulence, has occurred over longer cycles, with three or four outbreaks at most each century. Following data from various authors—such as Saillant (1780), Patterson (1986), Berche (2012), and others—we can conclude that Europe's most important flu pandemics and epidemics over the past three hundred years took place in the following years:

| | |
|---|---|
| 1729 | |
| 1732–1737 | |
| 1742–1743 | |
| 1761–1762 | |
| 1775 | |
| 1780–1782 | |
| 1788–1789 | |
| 1830, 1833, 1837 | |
| 1847–1848 | |
| 1889–1890: | An intense pandemic with a second wave in 1892 |
| 1900–1903: | Epidemic |

| | |
|---|---|
| 1918–1920: | Very intense pandemic (Spanish flu) |
| 1933–1935: | Epidemic |
| 1946–1947: | Epidemic (Italian flu) |
| 1957–1958: | Intense pandemic (Asian flu) |
| 1968–1970: | Pandemic (Hong Kong flu) |
| 1977–1978: | Pandemic |
| 2009: | Mild pandemic (A/H1N1 or swine flu) |

The mortality caused by pandemics during the twentieth century ranged from 40 million from the Spanish flu, 1 to 4 million from the Asian flu, and 1 to 2 million from the rest, except for influenza A, which officially caused only 300,000 deaths. In the following section, I will describe the Russian flu of 1889 because it marks the beginning of the long series of pandemics that have affected us in Europe and around the world over the last 130 years.

## 1889–1890 and 1892 Russian Flu: Epidemiology and Clinical Practice

One hundred thirty years ago, a new era began in which viral epidemics and pandemics became more significant. During the middle decades of the nineteenth century, the flu had moved into the background until, suddenly, in 1889, it moved to center stage once more. The origin of what was called Russian flu (1889–1890) may have been in China after the floods of 1888. Major epidemics were documented in Athabasca, Canada, in May 1889; in Greenland in the summer of 1889; and in Tomsk (Siberia) and Bukhara (Uzbekistan) in October 1889.

What we know for sure (Bertillon 1892) is that the first cases appeared in St. Petersburg, Russia, on October 27, 1889, spreading rapidly along railway lines throughout Europe. In Paris, the first cases were reported on November 17; in Berlin and Vienna on November 30; in London in mid-December; and, at the end of that month, in Southern European countries, from Italy to Portugal. It reached America by sea in mid-December 1889; the Cape of Good Hope and Suez in January 1890; Mumbai in February; Kolkata in April; and, by that time, the Russian flu was in Australia too. In other words, by the first months of 1890, it was already in the North and South America, Africa, Asia, and Oceania, reaching even the most remote islands, such as Madagascar, Jamaica, and St. Helena, by August.

In Paris, the first cases were benign and affected primarily department store, post office, and telegraph employees, and the like. I underline this fact because Paris was the most modern, cosmopolitan, and fashionable city in the world at that time. It received tourists from all over the world and, of course, the richest and most powerful families of Tsarist Russia enjoyed the city, shopped in the department stores, and lived in French culture and with the language as if they were their own. That is why it is worth considering the possibility that the flu virus arrived by train from St. Petersburg in the autumn, and the Russian clientele passed it to the employees of the *Grand Magasins* that were one of the initial focuses of the contagion.

As of December 15, the virus became extremely virulent, and mortality rose sharply. The period of maximum impact took place between December 16, 1889 and January 31, 1890, and it has been calculated that Russian flu caused 5,042 deaths in Paris. Most victims were over the age of 50, more men than women died, and the number of abortions did not increase. The crude mortality rate was 2.1 per 1,000 inhabitants (men 2.5% and women 1.7%). According to one recent study—Valleron (2010)—one million people worldwide died in the Russian flu pandemic, with a mortality rate of between 1 and 2.8 deaths per 1,000 inhabitants.

The Russian flu pandemic of 1889–1890 is surely the link between the epidemics and pandemics which took place during the Modern Age and the extremely virulent pandemic of 1918. Between the two pandemics, during the last decade of the nineteenth century and the first two of the twentieth century, there were multiple flu epidemics in many parts of the world, which doctors of the time saw as the remains of the 1889–1890 pandemic, eventually considering flu to be an endemic disease. These years are very important, and I am currently investigating the period of 1889–1894 and the responsible virus. It should be remembered that, at the time, flu pandemics were not differentiated from the seasonal flu, the winter cycle of seasonal epidemics was not known about, and the virus responsible for both the seasonal flu and the pandemic flu had not yet been discovered.

The clinical presentation of flu, in this first contemporary pandemic of 1889–1890, was different from the current clinical presentation. The *Académie de médecine de Paris* was the great temple of French medical knowledge, the most advanced in the world at the time. (Scientific sessions, open to the public, and hosting academic experts, are still held there to this day.) One of these academics, Achille Adrien Proust (1834–1903), a specialist in hygiene and professor of the subject at the *Faculté de medicine de Paris*, specialized in the evolution of epidemics.[9] With regard to the 1889 influenza, he published two articles in the Academy Bulletin (Proust 1892) on clinical forms of presentation of the disease, noting that, in many cases, the following three forms were intermingled:

- **Nerve flu.** Extremely abrupt start; very severe headache; very intense pains in the eye orbits; feeling of crushing in the eyes; very acute joint and muscle aches; sometimes accompanied by polymorphic rashes (scarlet fever, rubella, rashes on the forearms, wrists, and chest); sometimes

9 It should also be noted that he was the father of the novelist Marcel Proust (1871–1922).

hives. The set of symptoms observed in the flu revealed more of a general nervous disorder than an inflammatory state.[10]

- **Lung type.** The same features as with pharyngeal, laryngeal, and pulmonary determinations. This form of pulmonary congestion, angina, and pneumonia was undoubtedly the most serious form, and took place in all patients with complications. According to the report, complications were suffered mostly by those who had continued working or had gone back to work too soon; among those who, still suffering from the disease, had been subjected to cold; and finally, among individuals previously weakened by age or disease.

- **Gastric type.** Characterized by digestive tract disorders: vomiting, diarrhea, etc.

## 1997 Avian Flu (H5N1) in Hong Kong

After the Russian flu came the Spanish, Italian, Asian, Hong Kong, and other flu pandemics, until the end of the twentieth century. With regards to the last twenty-five years, we should highlight a very

10 "Les divers symptômes observés dans la grippe révèlent bien plutôt un trouble nerveux général, qu'un état d'inflammation franche, et les cas où ils présentaient ce dernier caractère étaient de beaucoup des moins nombreux." (The various symptoms observed in the influenza pointed towards a general nervous disorder rather than a simple case of inflammation, and there were many fewer cases in which the latter characteristics were found.) Proust, et al. (1892), 519.

significant outbreak which has led to an enduring research boom on pandemic and seasonal flu.

In Hong Kong, in 1997, a 3-year-old boy died from an acute respiratory case caused by a type A influenza virus that was only known to have caused an epizootic affecting birds: H5N1. The virus was transmitted among humans, causing 861 cases and 455 deaths (a mortality rate of fifty-three percent). This outbreak of avian flu was cut off with radical quarantine measures and the killing of all birds suspicious of carrying the virus. In following years there have been new outbreaks in countries in Southeast Asia, Asia, and Europe, all of which have been controlled in the same way.

In 2013, another influenza strain appeared, H7N9, with high lethality. Identified cases numbered 1,568, and 616 people died (a thirty-nine percent mortality rate). So, over the last twenty-five years, there have been different pandemics and epidemics caused by strains of the influenza virus (1997, 2009, and 2013), the coronavirus (2002, 2012, and 2020), and others of tropical origin such as AIDS (1980), Ebola (1976, with its largest epidemic in West Africa in 2015), Zika (isolated in 1952 in Uganda, Micronesia in 2007, and Brazil in 2015), and Chikungunya (which broke out around the Indian Ocean in 2006). This whole series draws a very worrying picture for the coming years, in which we must learn to live together and face this web of viruses and other emerging diseases.

Looking to the future, I would like to repeat that overcrowding, massive and widespread pollution of the planet, population movements through migration, work, or tourism (during 2019, 1.4 billion tourists and travelers moved around the world for their own entertainment), and climate change are causing a real cataclysm in our ecosystems and changes in many animal and plant species. These abrupt changes inevitably influence the microorganisms which, we must remember, are also part of our ecosystems—as we are ourselves too—and which coevolve with us on our planet. When we mistreat and destroy our environment, we become responsible for the changes induced in animals and plants, and even for the small changes in the genetic burden of a virus or bacteria that can end up causing a real cataclysm, such as that of SARS-CoV-2.

# Chapter 2
# Spanish Flu in Western Europe (1918–1920)

Seasonal flu epidemics kill mostly the elderly and the chronically ill. For example, the seasonal flu of 1916 in Madrid caused 183 deaths, 34.4% of which were people over 65 years of age. In Paris, in 1917, flu killed 127 people, of whom 41.7% were at least 65 years old. Most died in the first months of the year (twenty-seven in January, forty-five in February, twenty-three in March, and ten in April). The graph of all those who died from flu in 1917 in Paris (figure 2.1) is typical of seasonal flu epidemics to this day.

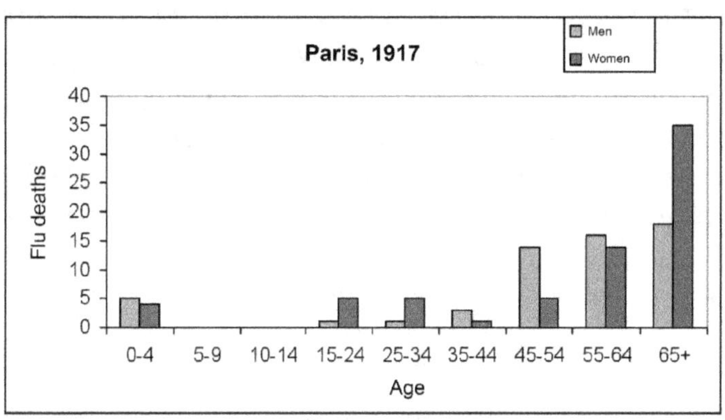


Figure 2.1. Age distribution of those who died from the flu in Paris in 1917. Source: *Annuaire statistique de la ville de Paris*.

## Hypothesis about the Origin of the Flu

The flu that broke out in the spring of 1918 is considered the first wave of the Spanish flu pandemic. There are several hypotheses on the origin of the 1918 flu pandemic: it came from China, spread by hundreds of thousands of workers who arrived in Europe and the United States between 1916 and 1918 (Ma 2019); it broke out in European military camps between 1916 and 1918 (Oxford et al. 2005; A. Erkoreka 2009a); and, it first appeared in U.S. military camps, being taken to Europe by the soldiers themselves on military convoys that sailed across the North Atlantic throughout the first months of 1918 and, above all, in the autumn of that year.

One way or another, the fact is that flu was already in Europe by the spring of 1918, with a very benign clinical presentation, affecting civilians and soldiers involved in World War I. Had this spring outbreak been the only one to take place, we would have forgotten about it by now. Today, one hundred years later, we would pay it no attention. In fact, we would see it as just one more of the seasonal flu waves that took place every year at that time, just as they continue to do so today.

## First Wave (Spring 1918)

In March 1918, there was a major flu outbreak among soldiers at military camps such as Camp

Funston (Kansas, USA) which Patterson and Pyle (1991), among others, consider to be the start of the Spanish flu pandemic. In my opinion, it is very difficult to give such an accurate date for the onset of the pandemic because there are previous outbreaks that could be linked to this pandemic, for instance the New York flu epidemic in February of 1918 (Olson et al. 2005). The narrative is also highly novelized (Barry 2005), even giving us a name for "case zero": a farmer in Haskell County, Kansas, the cook at the military camp, and the driver at the military camp—all of which makes it sound implausible. We can safely say that American and other troops involved in the Great War acted as spreaders of the flu pandemic, which started in April 1918 in both America and Europe.

Among the extensive documentation kept in the *Archives du Services de Santé des Armées* (ASSA), I found a "Note on flu in the army from April to November 10, 1918," in which it is stated that the first cases of flu were identified from April 10–20, 1918 in the Third Army at Villers-sur-Coudun, and in the training camp at Fère-Briange. Flu in the American army posted in France began around Bordeaux toward April 15, 1918. It was a benign fever epidemic accompanied by catarrhal symptoms, and American doctors believed that the etiological agent was Pfeiffer bacillus[11] (now called *Haemophilus influenzae*).

---

11 Haven EMERSON to Médecin Major RAYNAUD at Tours. "La grippe dans l'Armée Américaine" (Influenza in the American Army) (ASSA, volume 813) [originally in French] : "Towards the 15th of April an epidemic of benign fever with symptoms of catarrh broke out among American troops in the Bordeaux area.

This epidemic wave in the spring of 1918 was benign; it affected many soldiers but caused very few deaths. In this way, it was like a seasonal flu. The French military report notes that there were 24,886 flu patients in May, with 7 deaths; 12,304 in June, with 24 dead; and 2,369 sick in July, with 6 deaths diagnosed with "*grippe.*" Reports from American military doctors tell us that "influenza" cases among their troops added up to a total of 1,850 in April; 1,124 in May; 5,700 in June; and 5,788 in July, with the first five American soldiers dying from influenza that month (ASSA, Box 814).

It should be noted that among the Indo-Chinese troops stationed in France, there were also numerous outbreaks, which military doctors classified as "*pneumonie des Annamites*" (A. Erkoreka 2009a). These outbreaks are well documented in ASSA during 1916, 1917, and until the summer of 1918, as recorded by Darmon (2000) in Montpellier, Grenoble, and Rennes. From the symptomatology they describe, it can be concluded that these were cases of flu as corroborated by the military doctors themselves in an outbreak that occurred in Pau between the months of May and June 1918.[12] In Italy no significant increase in

From that time until the present day, that epidemic infection has continued to affect our troops to a greater or lesser extent in France and England. The benign character of the beginning of the epidemic led us to doubt that we were dealing with an infection caused by the Pfeiffer bacillus, but in mature cases carefully examined using bacteriological methods, in most cases Pfeiffer bacillus was found, and that has since been considered to be the unquestionable ethological agent."

12 "J'ai l'honneur de vous rendre compte que l'Ecole d'Aviation de Pau me signale 5 nouveaux cas de grippe chez des Indo-Chinois." (ASSA, volume 814)

mortality was detected during the spring of 1918 (Tognotti 2002).

The first country in Western Europe where the pandemic spread to large sections of the population, causing significant mortality, was Spain, especially in the city of Madrid (Porras 1997), which would justify the name of "Spanish influenza" by which this pandemic is known. The first reference to it was published in the newspaper *El Liberal* on May 21, and the following day *El Sol* was already talking about the disease affecting military garrisons and civilians, its symptoms being "headaches, chills, slackness, fever and joint pains, and disease sometimes causes chest and intestinal complications." Chowell et al. (2014) calculate, based on the epidemiological bulletins, that this wave caused excess mortality in Madrid of 1.0 per 1,000 inhabitants. By directly investigating deaths due to influenza and respiratory complications in the Municipal Archive of Madrid myself, I have calculated a rate for this spring wave of the flu pandemic of 1.7 deaths per 1,000 inhabitants for the months of May and June 1918 (see figure 2.2) (A. Erkoreka 2017).

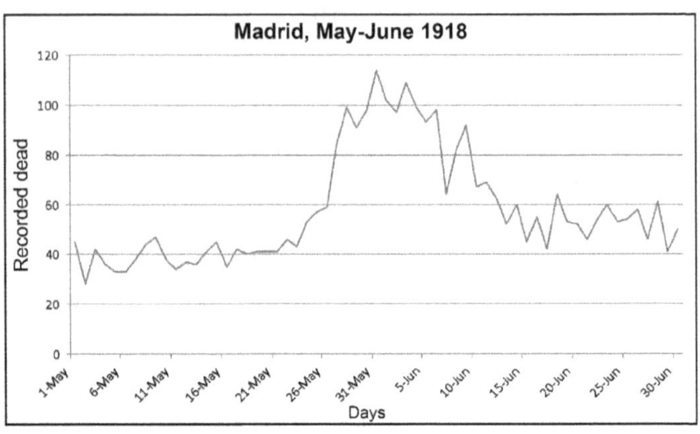


Figure 2.2. Deaths from all causes in Madrid from May 1 to June 30, 1918. Sources: *Archivo General de la Villa de Madrid*, and Piga and Lamas (1919).

Regarding the age of those who died from influenza in Madrid during the two months of May and June, 52.6% were between 15 and 44 years old, and the percentage of deaths of people over 65 fell to 12.3%. The graph of the ages of the deceased for this time period, only as a result of flu, has a *W* shape—typical of Spanish influenza—which leads me to suggest that this spring wave of 1918 may have been caused by a strain of the highly virulent influenza virus, similar to H1N1, which has been firmly identified as the cause of the second wave of the Spanish flu pandemic.

The spring pandemic wave arrived in Portugal from Spain in June, and lasted there until July. An official report of the time (Jorge 1918) on May 31 warned about the need to prepare for an epidemic which "*ameaçava imediatamente os concelhos da fronteira e os grandes centros.*"[13] On June 6, the pandemic was identified in the district of Porta Alegre, bordering with Extremadura in Spain. On June 10 it reached the city of Porto, and on June 11 Lisbon, with fifty cases in Monsanto prison. The report compares this outbreak to the pandemic of 1889–1890,[14] as does the note published by the Koch Institute in the *Berliner Tagablatt* on June 29, 1918.

In Spinney's interesting chapter (2018, 47–50) on "waves in a pond," he documents this first epidemic wave, during the month of May, in Breslau, Germany (now Wroclaw, Poland); in Odessa, Russia (now in Ukraine); in North Africa; reaching Mumbai in India; arriving in Japan; and appearing in July in Australia, after which it died down. He also cites that on June 1 the *New York Times* reported that "a rare epidemic plagues northern China," and that "there had been 20,000 cases in the northern Chinese city of Tiajin and 'thousands' more in Pekin."

The Treaty of Brest-Litovsk, signed on March 3, 1918 by the Russian Bolsheviks, took the country out of World War I and allowed Germany to move its troops to the western front. The Germans' offensive—*Kaiserschlacht* (the Kaiser's Battle)—failed miserably because, according to Spinney, 900,000 men were ill on the German side, as were

13 Translator's note. In Portuguese in the original: "Immediately threatened the town on the frontier and large cities."

14 "O seu carácter influencial, similar ao da pandemia clássica de 1888-1890 e da recente dos Estados Unidos (1915–1916)."

three-quarters of the French soldiers and more than half of the British.

The later famous psychoanalyst and thinker, C.G. Jung, managed an internment camp in Switzerland for people wounded in the war; the flu reached there in July. A few days earlier, the wife of a British officer interned there explained that the snakes in her dreams always meant diseases, and that she had dreamed of a huge sea snake. Jung regarded this as proof that dreams could be prophetic, including his own dreams (from weeks before the start of the Great War) of Europe flooded with blood that reached the Alps.

## Second Wave (Autumn 1918)

This was the wave that caused the greatest number of deaths worldwide, so I will call it the genuine Spanish flu pandemic. Its first appearance is well documented in the second half of August on the numerous military and civilian convoys that crossed the Atlantic (Schuck-Paim et al. 2012), and in three hot spots for the spread of the virulent new influenza virus: the ports of Brest (Europe), Boston (North America) and Freetown (Africa).

In Spain, the flu epidemic had disappeared over the summer, but in September it reappeared with digestive symptomatology in the initial cases. It was on newspaper front pages starting September

12;[15] the first health measures were taken on the seventeenth; the French border was closed on the twentieth; and the Portuguese frontier closed on September 30. The month of October saw the highest number of deaths, and the epidemic started to die down in November. Chowell et al. (2014) estimate that the excess mortality that occurred in Spain, due to all causes, in the three waves of 1918 and 1919, was 11.5 deaths per 1,000 inhabitants. They underline the great differences between provinces, the most affected being those of the northern plateau: in Burgos and Zamora 21.2 died per 1,000 inhabitants, and in Palencia 19.0 per 1,000. At the other extreme, the Canary Islands had a mortality rate of only 0.6 per 1,000 inhabitants. On the peninsula, the provinces least affected in autumn were those that had suffered from very intense spring outbreaks; Madrid, for instance, had had a mortality rate of 6.6 deaths per 1,000 inhabitants, Malaga 4.6 per 1,000, and Seville 5.0 per 1,000. Possibly part of the population had become immune after the first wave and therefore did not get ill in the autumn (A. Erkoreka 2017). Across Spain, just over 250,000 people died (Echeverri 1993), a ratio of 12.0 deaths per 1,000 inhabitants, as confirmed by Ansart et al. (2009).

In Paris, most of the deaths from flu were concentrated in October 1918, although the epidemic wave lasted from September to December, with a total of 7,777 people dying from the disease. It

15 *El Sol,* Madrid, September 12, 1918: "As soon as the temperature fell a little, the 'Soldier of Naples' epidemic, which was so successful last spring, has reappeared in Spain..."

is impossible to calculate the excess mortality in France because the country was immersed in the terrible Great War, and there is data missing. However, to find an approximate value for the actual impact of the Spanish flu pandemic, we can add together the people who died from flu and all respiratory system pathologies—which gives a mortality rate of 6.0 deaths per 1,000 inhabitants.

The age distribution of the deceased diagnosed with flu in Paris in 1918 is shown in figure 2.3, which is identical to the one obtained about Madrid. Those between the age of 15 and 44 account for 68.2% of the deceased, and those over the age of 65 account for only 6.4%. The huge difference between men and women is due to men of those ages having been called up and fighting at the front, so the number of women killed by flu is much higher: between the ages of 15 and 24, for example, 25.7% of the deceased were men, while the remaining 74.3% were women.

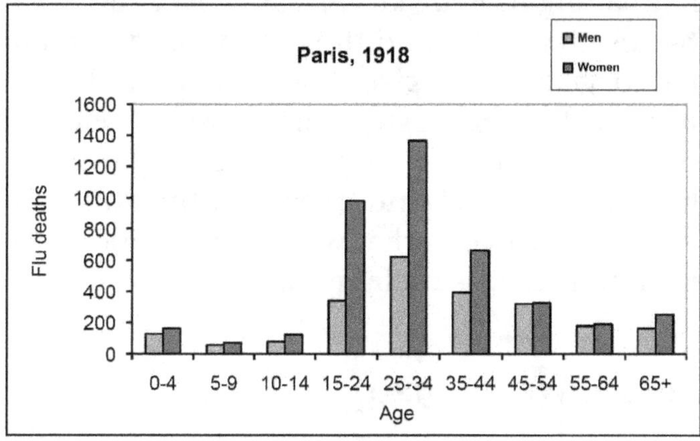


Figure 2.3. Age distribution of those who died from flu in Paris in 1918. Source: *Annuaire statistique de la ville de Paris*.

The mortality rates I have obtained for the whole of 1918 for Paris because of flu and respiratory complications are very low relative to other places (6.0 deaths per 1,000 inhabitants), as they are for Madrid (5.2 deaths per 1,000 inhabitants). We should take them into account, however, and consider them to be correct because there could be other factors at play, such as the prior immunization of the population—as mentioned earlier and with which I will deal again later.

## Third Wave (1919)

In Paris, the third flu wave took place between January and March 1919, with half of the deaths happening in February. Deaths over the age of 65 rose to 12.1%, and those between 15 and 44 fell to 57.4%. This gives the impression that the pandemic was losing strength because an increasing percentage of the population was beginning to become immune and, perhaps, the strains of the influenza virus that were in circulation were beginning to lose their virulence.

## Fourth Wave (1920)

In the first months of 1920 there was an outbreak which was the fourth, and final, wave of the Spanish flu pandemic. In Madrid, 467 people died from flu, most of them (311) in January. The same thing happened with respiratory diseases, which caused the deaths of 3,097 people in 1920, most of them (1,118) in January. The flu mortality rate plus respiratory system pathologies in January 1920 in Madrid were 2.2 per 1,000 inhabitants, which is the maximum figure which can be attributed to this last pandemic influenza wave in 1920. In terms of age, the number of young adults dying fell sharply: 38.6% of all deaths were between the ages of 15 and 44, and deaths over the age of 65 rose to 16.9%.

In Rome, between January and March 1920, 837 people diagnosed with flu died, most of them (578) in February. By age, according to the *Bollettino di Statistica del Comune di Roma 1920*, 34.6% of all deaths were between the ages of 20 and 40, and the deceased over the age of 60 amounted to 27.5%.

## Fifth Wave (1921)

Shanks et al. (2018) argue that in the islands and countries of the South Pacific, Spanish flu continued to spread until 1921, when the pandemic was completely eradicated in that part of the world. In Europe and America, there was no fifth wave of the Spanish flu pandemic and it finished there during the first quarter of 1920.

Throughout 1921, a total of 16,215 people died in Madrid (crude death rate from all causes: 23.8 per 1,000 inhabitants), of whom 209 were diagnosed with flu, with cases occurring mainly in spring and autumn. The distribution of deaths by age was identical to that of seasonal flu: 27.8% were over 65, and 15.3% were between 15 and 34. In Madrid, the cycle had finished, and the situation had returned to where it had been in 1916 and 1917.

In Paris, the 1921 curve was still relatively flat, with the percentage of deceased over 65 at only 14.5%. In contrast, during the following year, 1922, the graph looked like seasonal flu, similar to figure 2.1 for 1917, with 31.7% of deaths over the age of 65 (see fig. 2.4).

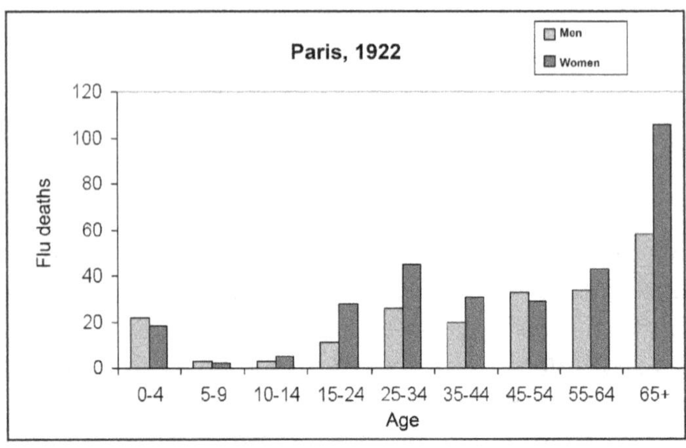


Figure 2.4. Age distribution of deaths from flu in Paris in 1922. Source: *Annuaire statistique de la ville de Paris.*

In summary, and returning to the Madrid data, the percentage of deceased between ages 15 and 34 from flu and respiratory complications went up from 12.0% in 1916 to 35.9% in spring 1918; down from 49.2% in autumn 1918 to 28.7% in 1920 and 15.3% in 1921. With regard to the *W*-shaped graph of deaths by ages, it is specific to the pandemic, as Simonsen (1998), Olson (2005), and others pointed out. These types of pandemic-specific graphs are very important for understanding pandemics' behavior and preparing for future flu pandemics, coronaviruses, and other viruses that will emerge in coming years. This feature (the *W* shape) has already been noted by Collins (1931) for the 1928–1929 epidemic, and by Viboud (2006) for the 1951 flu epidemic. It is clear that one of the groups most at risk for any future flu pandemic similar to the Spanish flu would be men and women from ages 25 to 34, followed by people between 15 and 24.

# Chapter 3

## Spanish Flu in the Basque Country

The Basque Country is situated between France and Spain. Its frontier position, the mountain range of the Pyrenees that separates the two states, the influence of the Atlantic Ocean in some areas, and the communication routes that run through the Basque Country from north to south between Paris and Madrid, give this small territory of 20,747 square kilometers and 1,272,645 inhabitants (in 1920) particular characteristics. In addition to human geography (anthropologists, geneticists, and linguists have studied the Basques because of their special characteristics and their ancient, non-Indo-European language), the territory has a unique physical geography and climate. The virulence of the virus, combined with the modes of transmission and vectors that characterized its spread within the Basque Country's unique region, resulted in a varying and contradictory development of the pandemic there.

We believe the Basque Country to be an interesting model for in-depth study of the development of the flu pandemic from 1918 to 1920 (as well as a better understanding of it), and one which can help us to understand pandemics that have subsequently affected us up until 2020, and pandemics which may appear in the future.

There was a first wave in the spring of 1918 which was very mild; a second, extremely virulent wave in the autumn; another mild third wave in the first months of 1919; and a fourth wave, which was almost unnoticeable, in the early months of 1920.

I will describe how the pandemic took place, placing special emphasis on mortality rates, the evolution of cases over time, and the Basque Country, as well as the notable differences between towns despite the small size of the whole territory. I will use some graphs to trace the spatial and chronological development of the disease, as well as the age of the deceased. In some cases, I will detail the characteristics of the first people who died in certain villages to make visible the people affected by the pandemic.

## First Wave (May–July 1918)

I have quoted three hypotheses about the origin of the pandemic which, in my opinion, can be combined; in each epidemic or pandemic outbreak, different strains that may have been mutating in China, around the war fronts in Europe, or in American military camps, all went around. Military camps were very poorly equipped since the US authorities had set them up too quickly train the two million recruits who had joined, and then move those recruits to Europe crammed into military convoys with deplorable sanitary conditions.

In Patterson and Pyle's account of the pandemic (1991, 7) they state, bluntly, that the pandemic arrived in Europe from the USA in April of 1918. According to these authors, the first cases appeared on the French coast around La Rochelle–Bordeaux, Brittany, and Le Havre in April, as well as in Italy, with Rome being the first city affected there. In May, the virus arrived in the UK through Glasgow, in Greece through Athens, in Albania through the south of the country, and in the Iberian Peninsula through Gibraltar, Cadiz, and Lisbon. I have ruled out the "landing" (by sea) of the virus in Lisbon (A. Erkoreka 2017) because Portugal was infected from Spain, the virus entering the country from Extremadura in June.

In my opinion, it is quite possible that the arrival of the new virus in Spain was through Gibraltar and Cadiz because some Andalusian and Castilla-La Mancha provinces were seriously affected, as was Madrid, which was the main focal point of this first wave. According to Chowell et al. (2014), the excess mortality attributable to Spanish flu in the spring of 1918 in the province of Cadiz (Andalusia) was 0.5 per 1,000 inhabitants; in Seville, 0.3 per 1,000 inhabitants; in Granada, 0.6; in Malaga, 0.2; and in Cordoba, 0.8. In Castilla-La Mancha, the figures were 0.6 in Ciudad Real; 0.6 in Toledo; and in Guadalajara, 0.4 per 1,000. Madrid, the epicenter of the first wave of the pandemic, according to Chowell et al., had an excess mortality attributable to the pandemic of 1.0 deaths per 1,000 inhabitants, although after carrying out a detailed count of the deceased, the rate for the months of May and June goes up to 1.7 per 1,000 inhabitants. From Extremadura (Badajoz, 0.4 per 1,000; Caceres, 0.3 per 1,000 inhabitants) the virus reached Portugal.

The pandemic wave affected northern Spain less, and we can say that it barely crossed the mountain ranges in the north of the peninsula, having no impact on Galicia, Asturias, the coast of the Bay of Biscay, the Pyrenees, and Catalonia. The only exception, as we will see, was Bizkaia (mainly Metropolitan Bilbao), which suffered a major outbreak in the spring of 1918, which Chowell et al. (2014) quantify at 0.6 deaths per 1,000 inhabitants. This same study, based on the epidemiological bulletins, does not show deaths from the first wave of Spanish flu in Araba, Gipuzkoa, or Navarre, although we have found deaths from flu in some civil and religious records.

In Vitoria-Gasteiz (Araba), for example, the Civil Registry only records the deaths of six people with flu diagnoses, all of them in June 1918. Specifically (to get an idea of the profile of the first deaths caused by the flu, and the rhythm of the pandemic), on June 8, a 22-year-old man diagnosed with "flu" died; on the fourteenth, a 12-year-old girl died, also diagnosed with "flu"; on the sixteenth, a 48-year-old woman died of "flu-related bronchopneumonia"; on the seventeenth, a 9-year-old girl with "flu" died; on the eighteenth, a 52-year-old man with "flu with endocarditis";

and on the twenty-third, a 38-year-old woman diagnosed with "flu-related pneumonia."

In Iruñea-Pamplona (Navarre), according to Ramos (1992, 120), the fifteen flu deaths in the spring of 1918 took place between May 10 and July 3. In Donostia-San Sebastián (Gipuzkoa) there were no deaths in this first outbreak of the flu pandemic. In the Northern Basque Country, there were no deaths from the pandemic in the months of June and July either. The civil records we examined from there do not show the cause of death. Although we detected a slight increase in mortality in Biarritz between March 26 and April 9, we do not know the exact causes of death.

In Bilbao, taking data provided by the *Boletín Mensual de Estadística Sanitaria de Bilbao*, we found that there was one diagnosed death from flu in May, sixteen in June, and three in July. Adding the forty-two deaths during these three months caused by pneumonia and bronchopneumonia, a mortality rate caused by Spanish flu of 0.6 per 1,000 inhabitants can be deduced. All the towns in the metropolitan area of Bilbao suffered equally from the pandemic. For example, in Erandio, the peak of the first wave was in June, the peak of the second, major wave was in October, and there was a minimal, third wave in January 1919.

At several places in the province of Bizkaia—for instance Durango (fig. 3.1)—there was a spike of deaths in the months of June and July, which doctors of the time put down to pneumonia and bronchopneumonia. I believe that this peak of deaths from pathologies of the respiratory system is highly significant, and that it shows the reduced presence of the flu epidemic, causing pneumonia and bronchopneumonia, as recorded by local doctors on the certificates. We can say with certainty that in the Basque Country the first pandemic wave had run its course by August.

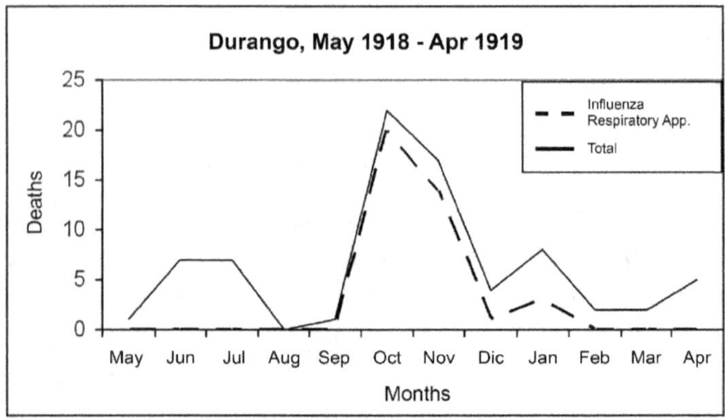


Figure 3.1. Deaths in Durango caused by flu and respiratory system pathologies. The spring and autumn waves of 1918, and the third wave of early 1919, are clearly visible. Source: *Parish Registry Books*.

## Second Wave (September–November 1918)

The month of August passed without alarm throughout the territory. On the *côte basque* in the French Basque Country there were very few tourists due to the Great War, while the peninsular coast was crowded with holidaymakers and tourists from many places in Spain.

During the first days of September, the weather changed, it started raining, and the flu reappeared. Newspapers of the time, after reporting the outbreak in Irun (Gipuzkoa) and Goizueta (Navarre), stated—as was to be expected—that the disease had come from France. Some documents I have examined in the *Archives du services de santé des armées* (French Army Health Services File, ASSA, Paris) talk about outbreaks in certain army camps in southwest France during the summer and, in some cases, consider the disease to have come from Spain. This is common to all pandemics and epidemics: they are attributed to other countries or groups—to the Spaniards, French, Portuguese, etc.

One of the mysteries that we Spanish influenza researchers have not solved is the simultaneous appearance of the second wave throughout the Northern Hemisphere during the first days of September. At that time, it appeared on the east coast of the United States, on the west coast of India, and in various places in Europe such as the Basque Country, on the border between France and Spain. The railway track width in Spain is different from the European track width, and all the Spanish trains stop at Irun to transfer to French trains waiting at Hendaia Station on the other side of the Bidasoa River. From there, trains left for Paris and all over France. So those two border towns were, and continue to be, a major communications hub; thousands of people passed through the hub daily, especially Spanish workers, and Portuguese workers and soldiers bound for France. Given that the flu virus originates with birds, it should also be noted that a variety of wildlife and migratory birds live in the marshes near Irun—currently Txingudi Nature Reserve.

The autumn pandemic wave started from this breeding ground, spreading, as we will see below, like waves when a stone falls into a pool. I will describe the development of the pandemic in the Basque Country, starting at Irun and Goizueta, and how it spread to the periphery of the territory like the ripples on a pond.

No one could have imagined at that time, in early September 1918, that the real Spanish flu was just beginning: the very serious epidemic wave which was to cause forty million deaths worldwide. This is the second mystery of Spanish influenza which, today, we are beginning to understand. The assumption now made is that the influenza virus mutated, and the H1N1 strain appeared, turning out to be extremely contagious and virulent. This strain of the virus was defined in the early twenty-first century, using tissues obtained from victims of the pandemic among the Inuit population of Alaska (Taubenberger, Morens, Fauci, Tumpey).

## Irun (Start of the Pandemic Wave, September 1918)

The disease appeared at the same time in several border towns in Gipuzkoa and Navarre, and the media of the time emphasized the extreme virulence with which it had appeared in Irun (Gipuzkoa) and Goizueta (Navarre). Preventive disinfection, health education, and isolation measures were taken in those two provinces, which even led to the border with France being closed on September 24.

The authorities attempted to downplay the development of the epidemic despite its scale and its extremely virulent effect on its victims: severe bronchopulmonary and gastrointestinal symptomatology which caused rapid death in a high number of cases. This was especially serious in closed communities such as military garrisons, which were affected from the start of this second epidemic wave.

Death certificates indicate high mortality from respiratory system pathologies, pneumonia, and bronchopneumonia at that time. In Irun, the first death occurred on September 5: a 24-year-old man diagnosed with "pneumonia." After half a dozen more similar cases, the first "*grippe*" (flu) diagnosis we found on record was a 25-year-old woman who died on September 10. As the month went on, the number of deaths increased to 11 on the twenty-second, and 10 on the twenty-eighth. Those figures are terrible in the context of a population of 14,161 inhabitants (1920 census). In September, 75 people in Irun were diagnosed with respiratory system diseases, and 16 were diagnosed with influenza and died. In October, from those same diagnoses, 41 and 7 people died, respectively. In other words, in those two months more than one percent of Irun's population died from Spanish flu. (The crude mortality rate for the whole of 1918 was 30.9 per 1,000, which means that approximately one-third of the deaths during those months were due to the pandemic.)

In the adjoining town of Hondarribia, at the very mouth of the Bidasoa River in Gipuzkoa, the first deceased person diagnosed with flu took place on the sixteenth, and the victim was a 27-year-old woman. On the seventeenth a 37-year-old man died, diagnosed with flu, and there was then an outbreak of cases: on September 19, a 42-year-old woman, a 34-year-old man, and an 18-year-old woman died of flu. A 58-year-old woman with chronic bronchitis and a 1-year-old girl with enteritis also died that day. As we have seen, there was a week's delay between the start of the pandemic in Irun and its appearance in neighboring Hondarribia. In that town, forty-two people died from flu and respiratory complications in September, plus another twelve from other causes. In October it was twenty-nine and fourteen, respectively.

In Irun, flu-diagnosed deaths were mostly among young adults between 15 and 34, who accounted for 41.0% of all the deceased. I would like to stress that the diagnoses of local doctors, as reflected in the records we have consulted, spoke in early September about "pneumonia" or "bronchopneumonia," and only as the epidemic progressed did they begin to certify the cause of death as a "grippe." In other words, these patients' symptoms were mainly connected with the respiratory system.

## Northern Navarre (Simultaneous Start of the Pandemic Wave, September 1918)

The other place where the pandemic wave started at the same time was in the mountainous area of northwest Navarre, bordering with Gipuzkoa—specifically in the small town of Goizueta. The reasons for this second simultaneous outbreak are not easy to determine. The people there work in agriculture and livestock, and it is not well connected to other communities. Jimeno Jurio (1977) gives a detailed account of the outbreak and development of the flu in this area of Navarre on the border with Gipuzkoa:

> The first cases were detected in Goizueta on September 3, a month in which many towns held their patron saint festivities in honor of the Virgin, the Holy Cross or Saint Michael. The press in Donostia-San Sebastián and Madrid soon gave alarmist accounts of the outbreak. The interior minister consulted with the civil governor of Navarre. On the afternoon of the 9th, Queipo de Llano travelled to Goizueta and Baztan with the provincial inspector of health, Dr. Jimeno . . . there were 200 people infected there, but no more than half a dozen dead.

We have examined the parish records of Goizueta (1,330 inhabitants in 1920),[16] verifying that in September, fifteen people died; in October, four people; and in November, one person (fig. 3.2). In other words, from September to November the mortality rate attributable to the second wave of the Spanish influenza pandemic was 15.0 per 1,000 inhabitants, which is more than 1% of the population. The media's report of half a dozen deaths is accurate because the parish book records, without indicating the cause of death, that from the third to the ninth of September, five males—aged 22, 34, 3, 18, and 5—as well as a 15-month-old girl, died.

16 I have taken population data about all towns of Navarre from the *Gran Enciclopedia de Navarra*.

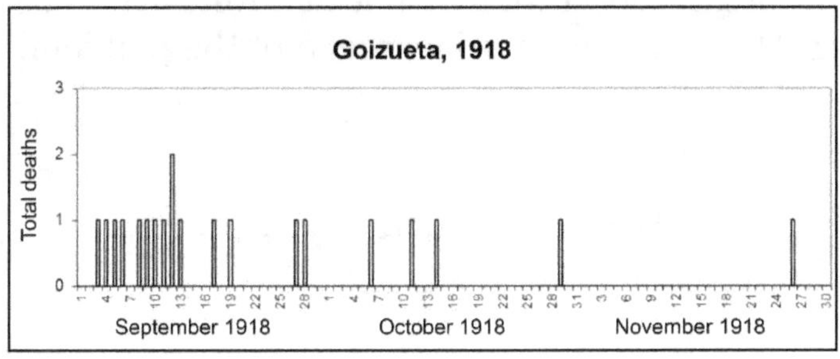


Figure 3.2. Daily deaths in Goizueta from September to November 1918. Source: *Parish archive.*

A little further north, on the frontier with France, is Bera (2,599 inhabitants in 1920), where, over those three months, seven, ten, and six people died, respectively, giving a mortality rate from the pandemic of 8.8 deaths per 1,000 inhabitants. To the south, at Leitza (1,695 inhabitants in 1920), over those three months, nine, eight, and one died, respectively, giving a mortality rate of 10.6 deaths per 1,000 inhabitants. Further south, on the natural communication route between Iruñea-Pamplona and Vitoria-Gasteiz, along the Sakana valley, the main town is Altsasu (2,669 inhabitants in 1920), where the disease arrived via the road between the two cities, and most deaths took place in October. Over those three months, nine, thirty-three, and three people died, respectively. The mortality rate for the second wave of the pandemic was 16.8 dead per 1,000 inhabitants. I would like to stress that despite the proximity of Goizueta and Irun to Altsasu, the mortality peaks were in September in the original focal points, while they were in October in Altsasu, so the initial spread of the pandemic was very slow.

## Etxarri-Aranatz (Mortality rate: 61.1 deaths per 1,000 inhabitants)

There is a town in the northwest of Navarre where the pandemic was especially virulent. Its mortality rate was the highest I have found anywhere in Western Europe; hence, I have researched it thoroughly. Etxarri-Aranatz (1,439 inhabitants in 1920) is in the natural region called Sakana-La Barranca—a long, wide valley between two mountain ranges, to the north and south, which is a natural communications route between the Iruñea-Pamplona basin and the Araba plain (east to west), and along which runs the road between Iruñea-Pamplona and Vitoria-Gasteiz. This important route intersects in Etxarri-Aranatz with the road between Donostia-San Sebastián and Lizarra-Estella. It is a Basque town with a compact, very well communicated nucleus, with local people working in livestock, agriculture, and forestry.

In 2008 I visited Etxarri-Aranatz's parish and its priests, Pello Etxabarri and Miguel Sagaseta, who made it easier for me to access the parish archive where I was able to examine the records and, above all, information about the deceased.[17]

17 *Libro de Difuntos de la Iglesia Parroquial de Echarri-Aranaz* (Etxarri-Aranatz Parochial Church's Death

According to the books, deaths from 1915 to 1917 were thirty-one, nineteen, and forty, respectively, each year. In 1918, 121 people died. Over the following three years, twenty-two, twenty-nine, and twenty-five people died, respectively. Most of the deaths in 1918 took place in October, when eighty-eight people died; in September, eight people died, and in November, seven. In the parish books, and specifically in the parish's *Libro de Matrícula* (Registry Book), the population was 1,120 in 1914, and 1,566 in 1925. Taking the population given by the *Gran Enciclopedia de Navarra* for 1920 as 1,439 inhabitants, the crude mortality rate for 1918 was 84.0 deaths per 1,000 inhabitants (the previous year it had been 27.7 deaths per 1,000 inhabitants). Taking into account only those who died in October, when the pandemic was at its most virulent, with eighty-eight people dying, the mortality rate was 61.1 deaths per 1,000 people. And in the three months we are considering, it was 71.5 per 1,000. In other words, we are looking at the highest Spanish flu pandemic mortality rate I have found anywhere in the Basque Country and throughout Europe.

Attempting to find out the cause of this high mortality rate—61.1 per 1,000 inhabitants, attributable to the 1918 flu pandemic—I also looked at the death rates for the late nineteenth century. In the aforementioned *Libro de Difuntos* (Death Register), covering the period of 1882–1920, I found that in 1887, thirty people had died from

---

Register), nº 6, 1882–1920.

all causes; in 1888, sixty people; in 1889, nineteen people; in 1890, twenty-nine; and in 1891 there was a total of thirty-three deaths. In other words, this data rules out the population of Etxarri-Aranatz having suffered from the Russian flu pandemic (1889–1890), and, therefore, it had no immunity to the flu pandemic virus. I must add that this is not a decisive fact, since probably other towns in this area of Navarre did not suffer from Russian flu either, and their mortality rates (for Spanish flu) are between 8 and 16 deaths per 1,000 inhabitants. There were also other seasonal influenza epidemics between the Russian and Spanish pandemics, some of which, such as in 1900 and 1907, were quite serious.

## The Rest of Navarre (September–November 1918)

Jimeno Jurio (1977) provides us with more data:

> By the 18th there had been numerous cases in almost the entire province. Orbaibar-La Valdorba was heavily affected, and the number of cases in Pamplona-Iruñea increased. By the end of the month, flu had taken over from Luzaide-Valcarlos to the Ebro Valley. There was widespread alarm. The press wrote about terrible cases and calls of distress. At Los Arcos, with

> a population of slightly more than 2,000 inhabitants, there were more than eight hundred people affected, including the doctor and the chemist; in thirty hours a dozen people had died . . . .
>
> Mendabia (2,781 inhabitants, 59 deaths, 2.12%), Artajona (2,541 inhabitants, 52 deaths, 2.05%) and Estella-Lizarra (5,144 inhabitants, 63 deaths, 1.22%) . . . In Pamplona-Iruñea there were 40 deaths during the month of September, 109 in October, and 61 during the first fortnight of November.

According to Ramos (1992), in Pamplona, between September 17 and November 17, 216 people died from flu. There was a major outbreak in the barracks and in the asylum, where fifty of the 520 patients died from flu. Statistics only show twenty-six deaths from flu at the provincial hospital and twenty-one at the military hospital, telling us that most flu patients were not hospitalized and died at home.

Finally, I present the data from Cortes (1,978 inhabitants in 1920), in the south of Navarre, in the Ebro valley, bordering with the province of Zaragoza. Spanish flu affected this population between the months of October and November, with four people dying from all causes in September, twenty-three in October, twenty-three in November, and two in December (fig. 3.3). The mortality rate from September to November was, therefore, 25.2 deaths per 1,000 inhabitants.

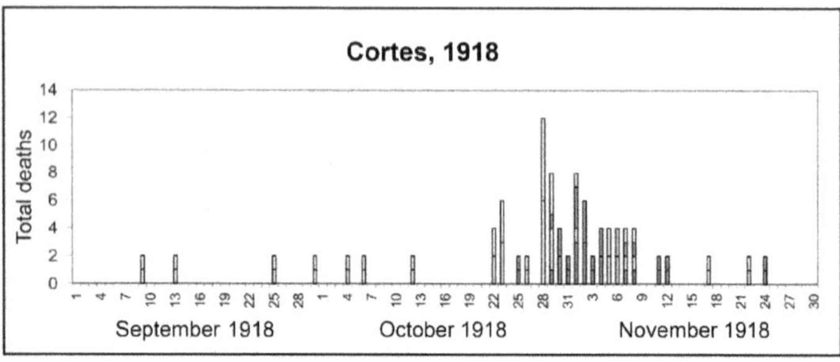


Figure 3.3. Daily deaths in Cortes from September to November 1918. Source: *Parish archive.*

The high mortality rates we have cited in some locations do not match the overall figures for Navarre calculated in a study about the whole of Spain (Chowell et al. 2014). This paper, based on official health bulletins, states that there was no first wave in Navarre in the spring of 1918 and that during the second wave, throughout the province, the excess mortality rate attributable to the pandemic was 9.2 deaths per 1,000 inhabitants. The low figures for Iruñea-Pamplona (32,635 inhabitants in 1920) are probably what led to the overall low figures of the whole province, where many towns were severely affected by Spanish flu.

I would like to underline the major differences from one town to another within Navarre. Large variations in rates exist, such as between Bera, in the north of the province (where 8.8 people died per 1,000 inhabitants) and Cortes, in the south of the ancient kingdom (where we estimate that 25.2 per 1,000 inhabitants died). I would also like to highlight the transmission speed of the pandemic. In early September there are good records about the flu in Goizueta and neighboring Irun, and it did not reach Cortes until the end of October. So, it took a month and a half to reach the Ebro valley in Navarre.

It should be noted that in October, concurrently, it appeared in most provinces and departments of Spain and France. I do not dare say, therefore, that the virus moved from town to town, like a stain of oil spreading throughout the territory. The impression I have is that the Spanish flu pandemic was synchronized, that it exploded at the same time in September in different parts of the Northern Hemisphere, and especially in October, but that also in November, it affected *all* towns and countries of the Northern Hemisphere. A compilation of the dates on which it began in the departments of France and in the provinces of Spain would confirm this.

## Northern Basque Country (September–October 1918)

Irun and Hendaia are two adjoining border towns, separated only by the Bidasoa River between France and Spain. The main communication route between the two countries goes through here, where the French and Spanish railway networks end, at Hendaia and at Irun, respectively. So it was a very important communications hub at that time, where Spanish and French travelers, Spanish and Portuguese workers going to or from France, as well as Portuguese soldiers going to or from the French war fronts (Portugal was an ally of France, while Spain was a neutral country) came into contact with one another.

At the same time as the second wave of the pandemic in Irun and neighboring Hondarribia, there was also an outbreak at Hendaia (population 4,632 inhabitants in 1921). The Death Register in the Hendaia Civic Archive, as is common to such archives in France, does not give the cause of death, giving only personal data, age, sex, and date of death. In September, twenty-nine people died: a mortality rate of 6.3 deaths per 1,000 inhabitants. On September 22, the epidemic reached its high point as five people were buried in Hendaia and ten in Irun that day, leading to the closing of the border on the twenty-fourth. If we add deaths in September to the eighteen in October, we see that more than 1% of Hendaia's population died, as in Irun, from flu and derived respiratory complications. It can be stated that the H1N1 flu virus was responsible because the graph of deaths by age has the typical *W* shape, and young adults between the ages of 15 and 44 made up 42.5% of all deaths in those two months of September and October.

While the pandemic appeared in September on the border between Hendaia and Irun, a few kilometers to the north, in Biarritz (population 18,353 inhabitants in 1921), the peak of the Spanish flu pandemic happened later, in October (A. Erkoreka 2009b). The highest mortality rate took place between October 8 and November 8, its peak on October 26, when seven people were buried. The thirty-six deaths in September, in addition to the fifty-four in October, would give a rate of 4.9 people per 1,000 inhabitants. In Biarritz there was a small increase of deaths in the first days of September, and the Spanish flu outbreak occurred in late October and early November.

I wish to make two observations about this. Firstly, French civil records do not give the cause of death. That is why, for Biarritz, we do not have the causes of death. There is, however, a first small increase of deaths between the third and the ninth of September; we do not know if that is connected with the onset of the pandemic. Secondly, and more importantly, it is from those dates onward that the number of deaths in Irun began to shoot up, and less so in Hendaia, the peak in both towns being on September 22. The development of the pandemic was different on the two sides of the frontier, rising much more sharply in the border towns in Gipuzkoa and Navarre than in those in France. Mortality rates were also much higher in the Spanish Basque Country than in the French Basque Country; in fact, in general the rates were much higher in Spain than in France.

To conclude our examination of data from the Northern Basque Country, the pandemic reached the inland villages, as well as the entire Pyrenean area, in November, which led to a very selective mortality. In the inland villages, the flu affected all the members of only a few houses, leaving other houses untouched. This information comes from personal communications with researchers Philippe Etchegoyhen and Michel Duvert in the Northern Basque Country. They even recorded testimonies from Spanish flu survivors, such as Paul Delpech, born in Sara in 1911, who claims that the flu had affected pregnant women much more, causing high mortality among them. Philippe Etchegoyhen also tells us that the 1918 flu killed more villagers than the Great War: "*La grippe avait tué plus de villageois que la guerre.*"

## Gipuzkoa (September–October 1918)

The second epidemic wave that began in Irun, reached Donostia-San Sebastián (67,281 inhabitants in 1920) in September 1918, with its peak in October, and disappeared in November. Over those two months a total of 735 people—1.1% of the population—died from the flu and its complications.

In Andoain, very close to Donostia, all the deaths caused by flu, and the few diagnosed only as respiratory system pathologies, took place in October, with the peak on the tenth. We have also studied two places in the Goierri area of Gipuzkoa:

Beasain and Lazkao, both on the road to Araba, the N1. The first fatal case of influenza appeared in these two places on September 11. Until the end of that month there were no more than a few patients, culminating in a mass of cases throughout the month of October, the disease abruptly disappearing on the twenty-ninth.

## Vitoria-Gasteiz (October–November 1918)

The main land communication route (road and train) between Paris and Madrid, went (and continues to go) through Baiona, Donostia-San Sebastián and, after traveling from north to south through the province of Gipuzkoa (N-1), reached Araba, crossing its capital, Vitoria-Gasteiz, and from there entering the province of Burgos (Castile) on the Madrid road.

The epidemic began to wreak havoc in the city of Vitoria-Gasteiz (34,785 inhabitants in 1920) at the end of September, and reached its maximum intensity throughout the month of October. It reached its peak on October 19 and 22. From the end of the month, and throughout the month of November, there were still a few cases; they continued to appear until the spring of the following year, 1919.

The pandemic wave progressed from north to south, crossing the Goierri area in Gipuzkoa, and with a month between its peak in Irun, on September 22, to its peak in Vitoria-Gasteiz on October 22. It used to be said that Vitoria-Gasteiz was a city of "soldiers and priests," emphasizing the demographic importance of these two groups that lived in their enclosed barracks and in the great seminary with young trainees from Araba, Bizkaia, and Gipuzkoa. The flu mainly affected young people between 15 and 24, followed by 25-to-34-year-olds, with more men than women dying. It should be emphasized that in our data collection a good number of deaths were among 21-year-olds, reflecting their status as recruits or seminarians. In that city, flu caused a reduced number of deaths among children and people over the age of 45, perhaps because some had been immunized by the mild spring wave or, in the case of the elderly, because they had been immunized by other pandemics and previous flu epidemics.

## Gipuzkoan and Bizkaian Coast (October–November 1918)

While the epidemic wave spread from north to south, from Irun to Vitoria-Gasteiz, in a continuous, clear, and forceful way, the same cannot be said of the spread of the pandemic along the coast. That must have been due to the abrupt terrain of the peninsular Basque coast and the difficult land communication between the coastal towns of Gipuzkoa and Bizkaia.

From Irun and Donostia-San Sebastián, it reached Zarautz at the end of September, where two people died from flu (the first, on the twenty-fourth, a 20-year-old man diagnosed with "*pneumonia grippal*"). During the month of October, twenty-four people with the same diagnosis died, and one person with respiratory pathology. Between November and April, a third, saw-shaped wave caused one to five deaths per month from flu and respiratory complications (fig. 3.4). In neighboring Getaria, eleven people died of flu and three died from respiratory pathologies in October, with only one more person dying from flu in November. In Deba, the westernmost town on the Gipuzkoan coast, five people were diagnosed with flu and died in October and, during that month and the next, there were three deaths caused by respiratory system diseases.

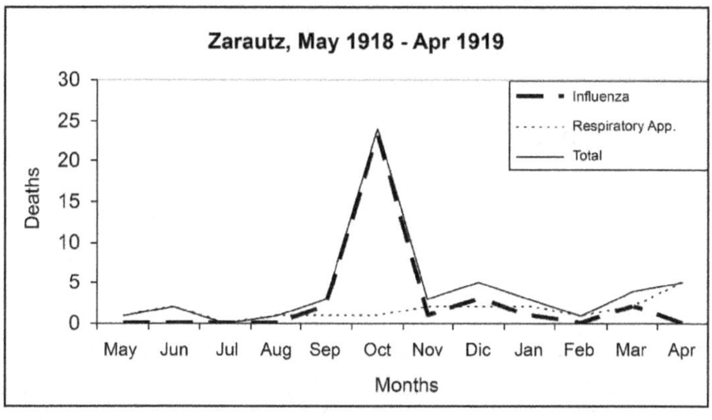


Figure 3.4. Flu and respiratory pathology deaths in Zarautz between May 1918 and April 1919. Source: *Parish archive*.

Bermeo, the main town on the Bizkaian coast, isolated between the sea and Mount Sollube, was mainly affected in November. In Bermeo (10,517 inhabitants in 1920) the spring wave had no mortality peak, but over the summer some cases of death from flu and respiratory complications were reported, and they increased progressively. In October, twelve people died; in November, twenty-three; and in December, eight. By January 1919, the flu had disappeared, although it made a reappearance, which was to be the third wave, with six flu and respiratory complications deaths, in February.

The last coastal town we have examined, Plentzia, also had a peak in November, probably coming from metropolitan Bilbao to which it was, and still is, well linked by train. The eighteen deaths from influenza and respiratory system diseases between October and November made up exactly one percent of the population.

## Mountain Villages (November 1918)

The highest summit of the mountainous area between Bizkaia and Araba is Gorbea, with an altitude of 1,475 m. On its slopes there are two towns, with their inhabitants scattered over different neighborhoods and hamlets, living in greater isolation than today because the communication routes were more precarious at that time. They are Zeanuri and Orozko. The epidemic arrived later in these places and lasted longer, beginning in mid-October and not disappearing until December.

The age of the deceased also had peculiar characteristics that should be highlighted: most were young children, between 0 and 9 years old, followed, as was usual in this pandemic, by young adults, between 25 and 34 years old. As elsewhere, the number of men dying was higher than that of women, especially in the age ranges of greater mortality. The mortality caused by the flu and respiratory system complications was the highest we have found in Bizkaia, reaching 25.7 deaths per 1,000 inhabitants from May 1918 to April 1919 in Orozko, and 24.1 deaths per 1,000 inhabitants in Zeanuri.

During 1918, the crude mortality rate due to all causes was much higher in Zeanuri (reaching 49.8 per 1,000) than in Orozko (38.4 per 1,000). These high numbers demonstrate the severity with which the flu affected these farming, livestock, and pastoral communities. Ander Manterola, a native of Zeanuri and the director of the *Ethnographic Atlas of the Basque Country*, has told me that in Zeanuri, details of the flu epidemic are still remembered with horror, as is how seven people were buried on a single day—an astronomical figure for a small rural town. In fact, local elderly people's memory is correct: the parish records we have examined state that on November 7 six people were buried, five of them diagnosed with influenza.

## Metropolitan Bilbao (October–November 1918)

From the data we have collected in Bilbao and in some towns around it, on both sides of the estuary, it is clear that the epidemic had a sudden outbreak in October which caused a great number of deaths, then decreased in November and almost completely disappeared that month, with only some isolated cases in early 1919. By age, the deceased belonged to groups which, *a priori*, should have been the strongest and the most resistant to disease: young adults between the ages of 25 and 34, followed by adolescents and young people aged 15 to 24, and children between 0 and 4 years of age. Deaths by gender were more evenly matched, although the number of men was greater than that of women (*Boletín de la Estadística Municipal de Bilbao*).

The pandemic wave arrived in Metropolitan Bilbao during the last days of September and may have come from the focal point in Irun, although other sea or land routes cannot be ruled out bearing in mind their role during the first wave during the spring. It progressed at such speed that it was already in Bilbao a few days after appearing in the towns on the Gipuzkoan coast and in Vitoria-Gasteiz, whose data and graphic we have already examined. In line with what we have already published on the Spanish flu pandemic in Bilbao (Gondra and Erkoreka 2010; Hernando 2021), I would add that in those years the major city in the Basque Country, Bilbao (103,172 inhabitants in 1918), had prospered because Spain had been neutral during the Great War, and there was trade with countries on both sides of the war from the port of Bilbao, which had produced a situation of economic euphoria (M. Erkoreka 2021).

The pandemic produced chilling figures in Bilbao. According to the *Boletín de la Estadística Municipal de Bilbao*, eight people diagnosed with "grippe" died in September; in October, 480 died; in November, 146; and in December, sixteen. The number of the deceased diagnosed with pneumonia and bronchopneumonia in these four months were 17, 138, 54, and 10, respectively. The total number killed by the pandemic—by flu, pneumonia, and bronchopneumonia—was 869, a crude mortality rate of 8.4 per 1,000 inhabitants for the months of September to December 1918 alone. The main characteristic of Spanish flu was that it mainly affected young adults (who made up 54% of the deceased) and young children (who were 15% of all those who died in those four months), as seen in fig. 3.5.

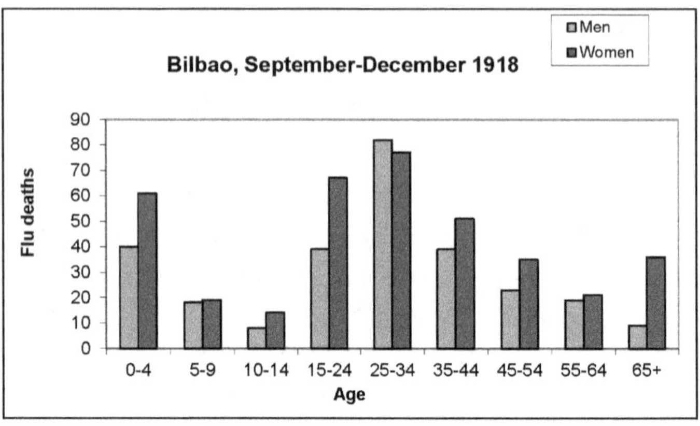


Figure 3.5. Ages of the deceased in Bilbao between September and December 1918; only those diagnosed with flu. Source: *Boletín de la Estadística Municipal de Bilbao.*

The autumn 1918 pandemic wave caused, as it did in cities all over the world, a true cataclysm. The Bilbao city council reinforced its municipal medical corps to care for those affected by the flu; all administrative and political authorities—local, provincial, and state—took anti-flu measures; the Academy of Medical Sciences published a pamphlet, in Basque and Spanish, with the prophylactic measures it advised for combatting the disease, and which we have republished[18] (A. Erkoreka 2006); the City Council of Bilbao published a

18 *Izurri-gexoa galazoteko Bilbao'ko Osalari-Bazkunak aginduten dauzan egin-bearrak* (Prophylactic instructions advised by the Bilbao Academy of Medical Sciences to combat the influenza epidemic). Bilbao: Bizkai-aldundijaren Irarrkolea = Imp. de la Excma. Diputación de Bizkaya, 1918. 8 + 6 p.

comprehensive report on the pandemic written by García de Ancos;[19] Deusto—which was a separate town at the time—also published an interesting economic report,[20] stating that the first case had taken place on September 26, and that a popular subscription had collected 21,829.85 pesetas which were used for family relief, the purchase of coffins, and fitting out a municipal sanatorium; and the religious authorities organized a great rogation day to the Virgin of Begoña, carrying her image in procession on October 27—attended by the authorities and an "immense crowd"—to the bridge of San Anton, Zabalburu, Gran Vía, and the Provincial Council, where the statue was shown to the public. The next day another mass procession took the image back to its sanctuary in Begoña.

## Mortality and Morbidity

To calculate the mortality of the Spanish flu pandemic in Bilbao, we will examine the annual

19 Ayuntamiento de Bilbao: *Memoria de la Organización y funcionamiento de los servicios municipales para combatir la epidemia gripal. Año de 1918.* (Bilbao City Council: *Recollection of the organization and operation of municipal services to combat the influenza epidemic. Year 1918.*) Bilbao, Imp y Enc. de José A. de Lerchundi, 1919.

20 Ilustre Ayuntamiento de la Anteiglesia de Deusto: *Memoria-Informe que las Comisiones Municipales de Beneficencia y Hacienda, han redactado para explicar el desarrollo de la grippe, y los medios que utilizó el Ayuntamiento para combatir la epidemia.* (Illustrious Town Council of Deusto Elizatea: *Report which the Municipal Charity and Finance Commissions have drafted to explain the development of the flu, and the means used by the Town Council to combat the epidemic.*) Bilbao, Imp. José Ausín, 1919.

period of maximum impact, which was between May 1918 and April 1919, taking into account, of course, all those who died from influenza, pneumonia, and bronchopneumonia. The total number of the deceased was 1,264, which is a gross annual mortality rate of 12.2 per 1,000 inhabitants for Bilbao, similar to what we have calculated for the whole Basque Country (12.1 per 1,000 inhabitants).

Regarding morbidity—the number of people who fell ill with influenza during the pandemic—García de Ancos estimates that in the province of Bizkaia (which then had a population of about three hundred thousand), two hundred thousand people fell ill with the flu. He estimates that doctors in Bilbao treated forty thousand patients, but considers this figure to be low, and thinks that the actual number of patients must have been higher,[21] and that many must have had mild cases of the disease without receiving any medical treatment.

In some small towns in the province, records about the sick were more detailed and reliable. For example, 1,000 of the 1,500 inhabitants in Lezama fell ill. The town council of Deusto estimated that 2,500 of its nearly 8,000 inhabitants had been affected by the disease (a number of patients which

21 To estimate the total number of those affected, García de Ancos examined the responses of Bilbao doctors to a circular sent by the College of Physicians at his proposal, to which 25 of the 141 professionals registered with the Sub-Delegation of Medicine answered, with an average of 273 patients per doctor having been treated. Extrapolating this relationship to the total number of practicing doctors is how García de Ancos arrives at the estimate of forty thousand attended to for influenza.

we believe to be much lower than what must have been the real figure in the town). The data provided by the military authorities of Bilbao recorded 488 soldiers being affected, of whom 16 died, from the total of 1,220 soldiers who made up the entire garrison.

Clearly, the number of people affected by the pandemic was very high, and we can say with certainty that more than 50% of the population of Bizkaia became ill over the course of the four waves of Spanish flu.

## Some Exceptions

In riverside towns on the Gernika-Mundaka estuary—now part of the Urdaibai Biosphere Reserve—then, as now, there was an enormous diversity of migratory birds and all kinds of wildlife living in its marshes, and the epidemic developed in a different way there compared with the rest of the territory. There was no first epidemic wave in late spring 1918, and the second wave was of low virulence, taking place between September and November. But from January 1919, during what we can consider to be the third wave (see fig. 3.6), the epidemic really broke out and reached its peak in February, decreasing significantly in March, and disappearing completely in April. The number of female children affected was higher than the number of male children, and that of young men was higher than that of women.

It should also be said that in some places we have examined, such as Aia, on the Gipuzkoan coast, flu deaths were very low (the gross influenza mortality rate was only 2.2 deaths per 1,000, while the flu rate plus respiratory diseases rose to only 7.5 per 1,000). In Deba, a Gipuzkoan coastal town bordering with Bizkaia, there was a similar situation.

Even in a small town, such as Zerain, and in some villages in Navarre and Bizkaia, there was no pandemic at all, and local people were able to organize themselves and take isolation measures that prevented the spread of the flu; they managed to not be affected by it, becoming true *safe villages* (A. Erkoreka 2020).

## Third Wave (January–May 1919)

Studies such as Johnson's (2003, 134) on England, Scotland, and Wales clearly and without leaving any doubts show the three pandemic waves. In our case, in the Basque Country, the third outbreak did not take the form of a typical pandemic wave. Instead, it moved in no particular direction, and was dispersed and irregular, as if it were a mere outbreak of the pandemic that appeared especially in the first months of 1919.

In the civil register at Vitoria-Gasteiz—where we have examined all the causes of deaths for the year—at the beginning of the year there were cases described simply as "*grippe*" (influenza), but there were also cases of "flu with complications," and sometimes, in greater detail, "flu complicated with bronchopneumonia" or similar diagnoses. In other words, doctors were aware that the flu caused respiratory, digestive, and other organ complications, and reflected that on the death certificates they drew up. In Vitoria-Gasteiz there were at least ten deaths in January diagnosed as being caused by "*grippe*," nine in February, seventeen in March, and five in the first days of April. There were also a dozen flu deaths in Irun between January and April, along with a high number of cases of pneumonia and bronchopneumonia. We have also seen that, in other towns during the first quarter of 1919, there were flu deaths—such as the six in Bermeo in February, three in March in Zarautz, and many others, which can be seen in figure 3.4. In the Northern Basque Country, we have found no trace of this third wave in Biarritz (A. Erkoreka 2009b) or in other towns along the *Côte basque*.

In Bilbao, the *Boletín Epidemiológico* mentioned previously reflects a more serious situation and informs us that between January and May 1919, a total of 329 people died from flu, pneumonia, and bronchopneumonia, which gives a crude mortality rate of 3.1 per 1,000 inhabitants. In other words, Bilbao's is a significant and important number that shows us this third wave was a major event in that industrial city.

In what is currently the Urdaibai Biosphere Reserve, the pandemic took on a different shape compared with the rest of the territory. The second pandemic wave in autumn 1918 was not very intense. On the other hand, the third wave was significant in places such as Gernika and Busturia (fig. 3.6). In the latter town, seven people died of flu in February, and there are also records of people having died there in May 1919.

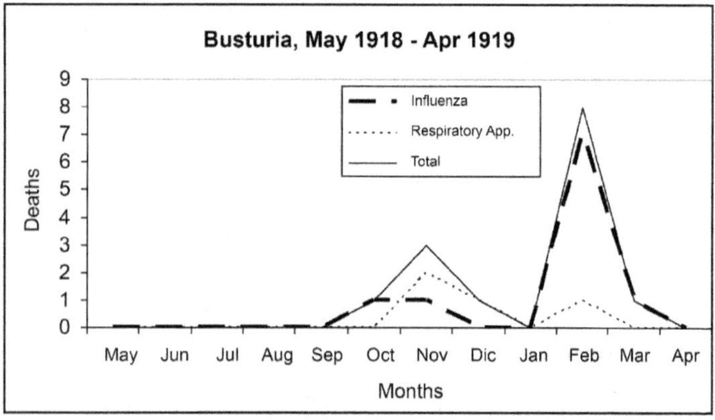


Figure 3.6. Deaths from flu and respiratory pathologies in Busturia, between May 1918 and April 1919. Source: *Parish records.*

In some towns further away from the main communication routes, on the slopes of the mountains (where the second pandemic wave was delayed until November, and in some cases even until December), the new wave in 1919 was also delayed. In Zeanuri, for example, the epidemic escalated in the spring of 1919, with most deaths from flu occurring in April, and the disease completely disappearing in May. Interestingly, in some of the small towns we have examined, such as Abadiño (in Bizkaia), the flu epidemic is still called "the 1919 flu" (*1919garren urteko gripea*) and not the "flu of 1918," which is more common.

## Fourth Wave (First Half of 1920)

There was a fourth wave of the Spanish flu pandemic in the early months of 1920. Echeverri (1993, 94) states that in the Spanish state it mainly affected children under 1 year of age, and that it caused the deaths of 17,841 people. He believes that happened because they were "the only part of the population who totally lacked immunity against the flu virus that had made its appearance in the spring of 1918."

In some places in Bizkaia, we have identified deaths from flu in the months of March and April, accompanied by a series of respiratory diseases such as pneumonia and bronchopneumonia, and some outbreaks of measles with bronchopneumonic complications. In Bilbao, data from the *Boletín Mensual de Estadística Sanitaria de Bilbao* confirms that the fourth wave took place between January and March 1920, causing the deaths of 65 people because of flu and 182 because of pneumonia and bronchopneumonia. So, the mortality rate was 2.2 per 1,000 inhabitants. Although the sample is small, it is significant that this graph still has a *W* shape, indicating, possibly, that some strain or variant of H1N1 was still circulating in Europe: 35.4% of the deceased were between 25 and 34 years old and 23.1% were between 0 and 4 years old.

In Europe, the Spanish flu pandemic is considered to have finished in 1920, and the 1921 and following flu cases were considered seasonal and not pandemic influenza. As I stated in chapter three, Shanks et al. (2018) believe that there was a fifth wave in the South Pacific in 1921.

# Chapter 4

## Spanish Flu Mortality Rates

We must start by saying that, in the Basque Country, there was hardly a first wave at all, with the only exception being the industrial Bilbao area. If that had been the only outbreak, it would have gone unnoticed, viewed as a seasonal epidemic like those that happen every winter. We would have seen the third and fourth waves in the same way, considering them to be no more than a series of cases in the first months of 1919 and 1920.

Taking a random sample of twenty-one towns in the Basque Country that, in 1920, had a total of 129,696 inhabitants,[22] I have calculated rates and produced graphs that summarize what happened throughout the Basque Country. Starting with fig. 4.1, we see clearly that the Spanish flu pandemic affected the Basque Country between September and November 1918, with most deaths taking place in October. It is also clear that there was a slight first pandemic wave around June 1918 and another, lesser, third epidemiological wave around March 1919.

22 Aia, Andoain, Basauri, Beasain, Bermeo, Busturia, Durango, Erandio, Ermua, Errigoiti, Galdakao, Gernika-Lumo, Getaria, Irun, Lazkao, Orozko, Plentzia, Santurtzi, Vitoria-Gasteiz, Zarautz, and Zeanuri.

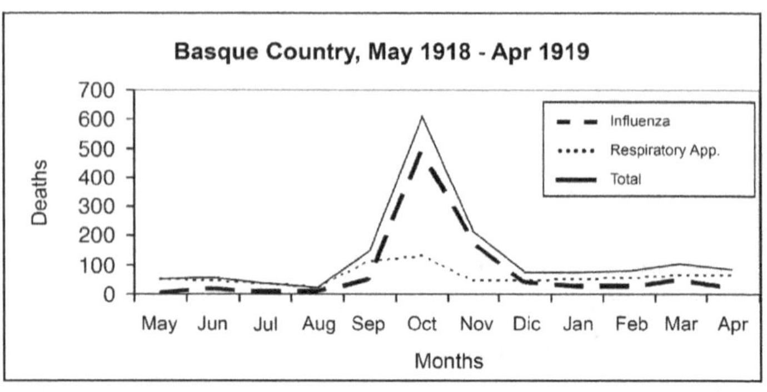


Figure 4.1. Monthly distribution of deaths from flu in the Basque Country, from May 1918 to April 1919. Source: *Church and civil archives from twenty-one Basque towns and cities.*

## Number of Deceased per Wave

I confirmed that there were four pandemic waves in Bilbao, the largest city in the Basque Country in 1918. I have taken my data from the very reliable *Boletín de la Estadística Municipal de Bilbao*, which allows us to examine deaths by wave to get an idea of the virulence of each of them in the city. This data about the virulence of the different waves can be used to compare with other pandemics caused by similar viruses, such as Hong Kong flu in 1968, COVID-19 in 2020, and other viral pandemics that will arise in future years. It should be remembered, for example, that the Hong Kong flu that killed one million people half a century after Spanish flu, had a very mild epidemic first wave in the winter of

1968–1969, and a very virulent second wave that hit Europe in December 1969.

Returning to Bilbao and taking into account all the deaths caused by flu, pneumonia, and bronchopneumonia (but leaving aside pulmonary tuberculosis, chronic bronchitis, acute bronchitis, and other respiratory complications), we know that between May and July 1918, 62 people died; between October and December 1918, 869 died; between January and May 1919, 329 died; and between January and March 1920, 247 people died. This gives a total of 1,507 people in Bilbao who died from the 1918–1920 influenza pandemic.

The following list shows the percentages of deaths during each of the waves:

| | |
|---|---|
| First wave (spring 1918) | 4.1% |
| Second wave (autumn 1918) | 57.7% |
| Third wave (first months of 1919) | 21.9% |
| Fourth wave (first months of 1920) | 16.3% |

As we can see, the death toll during the second wave of Spanish flu in Bilbao was fourteen times higher than during the first wave. The greatest severity of this second wave was the same in all the places and countries I have studied. However, there were different degrees of intensity: for example, in Madrid, the second and third waves together caused four times more deaths than the first; in Burgos there were eight times more dead in the second and third waves combined than in the first; and in Seville, ten times more than during the first wave (Chowell et al. 2014). In Bilbao, the third wave was of lower virulence, and only caused five times more deaths than the first wave. And the last wave, in 1920, was only four times more virulent than the first. Furthermore, with regard to the last two waves, it should be noted that what occurred was a steady number of deaths over several months, like fine rain over a very long period, and not an accumulation of cases during a single month (which was what had happened during the first two waves).

## Age and Sex of the Deceased

Taking this sample from twenty-one places with 129,696 inhabitants, figure 4.2 shows the distribution of deaths by age, and it is very clear that the flu affected young adults more than any other age group. Of the deaths, 24.5% were between the ages of 25 and 34; 17.7% were adolescents and young people between 15 and 24 years of age; 15.7% were children between 0 and 4; and there was a significant number of deaths (13.6%) of people aged between 35 and 44. In other words, 55.8% of all deaths in the Basque Country were between the ages of 15 and 44. The rest of the population—

children, older adults, and the elderly—suffered less from the 1918–1920 flu pandemic outbreak.

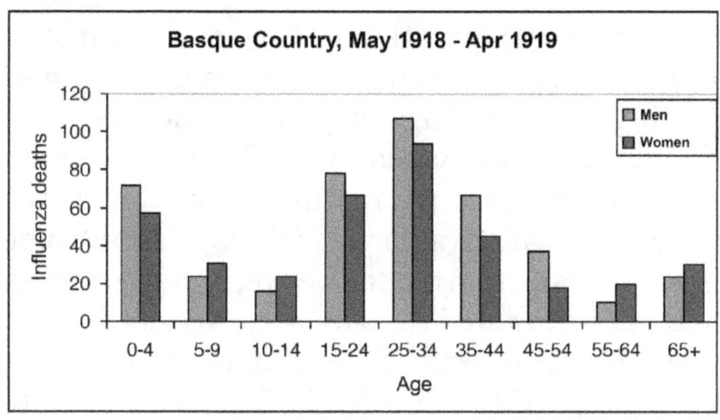


Figure 4.2. Age distribution of deaths from flu in the Basque Country. Source: *Church and civil archives from twenty-one towns and cities.*

By gender, 53.0% of those who died from flu were men, and 47.0% were women. By age, men and women were fairly balanced between the ages of 15 and 34, while the biggest differences occurred between the ages of 35 and 54, when significantly more men than women died. It is interesting to note that in all deaths caused only by respiratory pathologies, the proportion is more balanced, with 51.6% men compared to 48.4% women.

## Average Age of the Deceased: 28 Years Old

On further examination of the same sample of 129,696 inhabitants in the Basque Country and putting in order of age only those who died from flu between May 1918 and April 1919, we obtain the graph in figure 4.3, in which we see that in the female population (as in the male population) there is no plateau of flu deaths between the ages of 25 and 34, but there is a peak at 31 years of age. A second, similar peak occurs with 1-year-olds. The average age of all these deaths from only flu is 28.

Twenty-eight is a very significant figure because the previous Russian flu pandemic had affected the Basque Country at the beginning of 1890—in other words, exactly twenty-eight years earlier. This means that the deceased of that age and up had already lived through the Russian flu, which had not had a major impact in the Basque territory.

The data about 28-year-olds which I have found in the Basque Country is consistent with that used by Viboud et al. (2013) which, in a sample of the North American population, estimates that the average age of those who died from influenza in the 1918 pandemic was 26 years, and with that of Gagnon et al. (2013) which also calculates an average age of 28 years and links that finding that with the pandemic of 1889–1890.

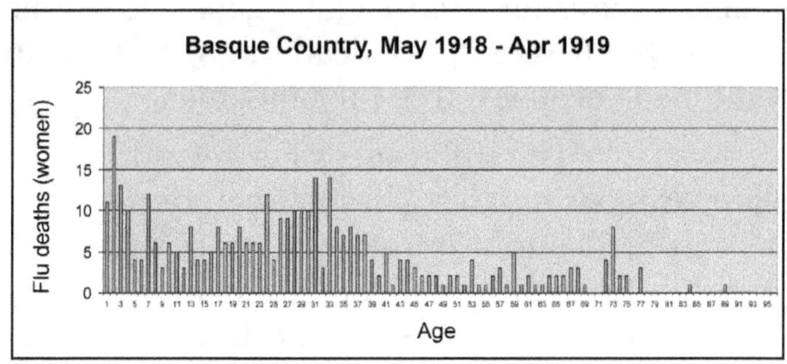


Figure 4.3. Ages of women who died of flu in the Basque Country. Source: *Church and civil archives from 21 towns and cities.*

## Crude Mortality Rate: 12.1 per 1,000 Inhabitants

The crude mortality rate per thousand inhabitants per year, in this sample of 129,696 inhabitants of the Basque Country, between May 1918 and April 1919, gives 6.8 per 1,000 inhabitants for deaths diagnosed as caused by flu. For all flu-diagnosed deaths, plus those diagnosed with related respiratory complications (pneumonia and bronchopneumonia), the crude mortality rate is 12.1 deaths per 1,000 inhabitants per year. I have excluded pulmonary tuberculosis from this count because it was a widespread pathology in both the industrial and rural areas of the Basque Country, causing a great number of deaths that would skew (and artificially raise) mortality rates. In absolute numbers, the estimate is that throughout the Basque Country there were 15,399 deaths in 1918 and 1919 combined because of the flu pandemic.

The differences between different places are considerable. The lowest crude mortality rates from flu and respiratory diseases have been found in towns in the French Basque Country (A. Erkoreka 2009a), where I estimate that the mortality rate attributable to Spanish flu was around 6.2 deaths per 1,000 inhabitants. In the Spanish Basque Country, the town with the lowest mortality rate I have found was Aia (Gipuzkoa), with 7.5 deaths per 1,000 inhabitants, and the highest rate of influenza mortality and respiratory complications found was in Etxarri-Aranatz (Navarre), with 61.1 deaths per 1,000 inhabitants.

The crude mortality rate, for all causes of death and for the whole year of 1918, is of great interest, and it, too, shows notable differences from one place to another.

| City/Town | Crude Mortality Rate (per 1,000 inhabitants) in 1918 |
|---|---|
| Aia | 16.2 |
| Côte basque | 21.9 |
| Vitoria-Gasteiz | 29.2 |
| Zeanuri | 49.8 |
| Etxarri-Aranatz | 84.0 |

## Effect of Spanish Flu Pandemic on the Economy

According to a recent study by Mikel Erkoreka et al. (2021), the Basque Country shows a dual starting stage with regard to the emergence of the pandemic. Although less intensely than in other territories within the French state, the Northern Basque Country had suffered the demographic and economic consequences of World War I, facing the pandemic after four bloody years of war. The provinces in the Southern Basque Country, on the other hand, had benefited from Spanish neutrality during World War I. The pandemic reached Bizkaia, Gipuzkoa, Araba, and Navarre at the end of a cycle of economic expansion. During World War I, the profitability of Basque industry—mainly in Bizkaia and Gipuzkoa—had increased dramatically with increased sales due to reduced competition in the European market. The extraordinary increase in profits during the war had also led to an exponential increase in the public administrations' tax revenue. So, companies and public administrations in the Southern Basque Country faced the impact of the pandemic with considerable financial resources.

The first three waves of the Spanish flu pandemic took place at the end of World War I and during the resulting economic crisis that Bizkaia went through because of having to adapt its industrial production to the new international scenario of peace. Contemporary business sources show that the main problem of companies in Bizkaia and Gipuzkoa in the autumn of 1918 and the spring of 1919 was not the impact of the pandemic, but, rather, the radical adjustment of war economies to peacetime, and growing social tension caused by sharp price rises. Spanish flu still led to considerable social alarm and, especially during the second wave, panic (as reflected by the media of the time, the public administration measures that were taken, and oral testimony that has endured to this day).

## Summary in the Basque Country

In the Basque Country, the Spanish flu pandemic had an abrupt onset, it caused major social alarm, and more than half of the population became ill. The death toll from influenza, pneumonia, and bronchopneumonia was 12.1 people per 1,000 inhabitants, which, in absolute numbers, accounted for just over 15,000 people between 1918 and 1919. The first wave was benign and did not affect the entire territory, the second wave was very sharp and very serious, and the third and fourth waves lasted for several months, causing a smaller number of on-going deaths. The average age of all flu-diagnosed deaths was 28, with 25-to-34-year-olds being the most affected age group. Economics and society did not suffer as much in the Southern Basque Country as in the Northern Basque Country because of Spain's neutrality during the Great War and the resulting cycle of economic expansion.

## Spain: 250,000 Estimated Deaths

The population of Spain was 20,880,000 (1920), and, according to official data from the Geographical and Statistical Institute, the flu pandemic of 1918–1919 resulted in the deaths of 182,865 people. Chowell et al. (2014), examining excess flu mortality and respiratory system pathologies, estimate that between May 1918 and April 1919 between 194,960 and 237,600 people died. From Navarro's collection of health data (2002), it can be calculated that, in 1918 and 1919, 213,337 people died of flu and respiratory pathologies (fig. 4.4). Echeverri (1993) raises the figure to 257,082 dead, or 12.0 per 1,000 among the population of Spain. Ansart et al. (2009) accept this estimate of excess mortality from the Spanish flu pandemic of 12.0 per 1,000 inhabitants for 1918 and 1919. In my opinion, this is the most accurate estimate: between 250,000 and 260,000 people died in Spain from the 1918–1919 flu pandemic, with large variations from one province to another. The provinces of the northern plateau were the hardest hit (from Burgos to Zamora), and the Canary Islands were the least affected.

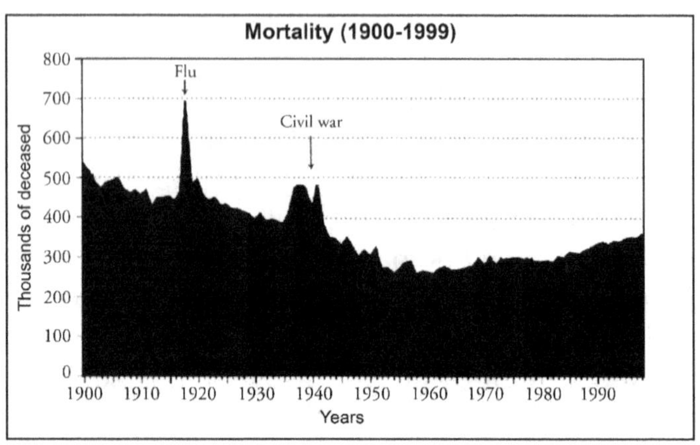


Figure 4.4. Number of deaths in Spain, year by year, throughout the twentieth century. Spanish flu deaths, Civil War, and post-war repression deaths stand out. Source: Navarro, 2002, 51.

## Mortality Hypothesis in France

In France (36,637,000 inhabitants in 1921), the number of people killed by Spanish flu that has traditionally been given is 137,200: a death rate of 3.7 per 1,000 inhabitants. Darmon (2000), using a very literary title to underline the pandemic's link to World War I ("A tragedy within a tragedy"), speaks of 210,900 dead, while Zylberman (2003)—competing with the drama in the title of his article, "A Holocaust within the Holocaust. The Great War and the Spanish influenza epidemic in France"—gives a total of 240,000 dead (7.3 per 1,000 inhabitants). Ansart et al. (2009) give the same estimate of excess mortality of 7.3 deaths per 1,000 inhabitants.

I have underlined the titles of the articles of the latter two French authors because World War I was a holocaust and a tragedy for that country, and it still remembers it with memorials and commemorative plaques in all its towns and cities. Possibly those connotations of tragedy connected with the holocaust of the Great War have been one of the reasons why in France there are only very limited studies or local theses on the subject, and very few systematic, overall investigations into the 1918 influenza pandemic. My impression is that French researchers have held back on this subject, and that in-depth studies are needed because that rate of 7.3 deaths per 1,000 inhabitants due to flu and its respiratory complications seems, at first glance, very low.

In my forays into the Municipal Archives of Paris, Pau, Biarritz, and some small towns in the Northern Basque Country, I have been able to verify that, in fact, the rates I have obtained from that original data are lower than in Spain or Italy. In the whole of the Basque Country, where I followed the same methodology to carry out my study, I also found clear differences between the figures obtained in the northern (French) region and the southern (Spanish) region.

To attempt to explain these differences, I want to raise a first hypothesis that not many French men who died or disappeared at the front were on the census at the time, and that they joined it after the war, starting in 1920, so they are therefore not accounted for in death tolls. In some local files I examined, I corrected the data later, adding it to the year of the war in which they died; however, that did not substantially change the final rates.

A second hypothesis I raise is that the French population was immunized by the spring flu epidemic or, more likely, by previous epidemics, and that therefore, they did not suffer as much from the second wave of Spanish flu. It would be comparable to what happened in Madrid, where there was a very low second wave when compared to other Spanish provinces (A. Erkoreka 2017). This would mean that some strains of the influenza virus circulating between soldiers and civilians, at least in 1916 and 1917, were related to H1N1, which was responsible for the second epidemic wave in 1918. This would confirm that the outbreaks at the military camp at Étaples—examined in depth by Oxford et al. (2002, 2005, . . . 2020)—were at the origin of Spanish flu, as was pneumonia affecting "indigenous" troops (A. Erkoreka 2009a).

I think the role of Indo-Chinese soldiers and workers from the ancient kingdom of Annam (now Vietnam, Laos, and Cambodia) who fought on French soil is important. Frémeaux (2006) and Van Ho (2014) point out that France brought 50,000 Indo-Chinese from its colony, half of whom went to *bataillons d'etapes*. Of these, 9,000 Annamites served as nurses, and 5,000 as car and truck drivers. In the *Archives du services de santé des armées* in

Paris (ASSA), I found many references to periodic epidemics affecting these Indo-Chinese soldiers and workers between 1916 and 1918 (A. Erkoreka 2009a). In military medical reports, they are given names such as "*pneumonie des Annamites*" and "*infections à pneumocoques.*"

A very interesting outbreak of this "Annamite pneumonia" is described in a report by military physician Cachie on May 13, 1918, describing the symptoms of affected Indo-Chinese soldiers from April 30. The literal text,[23] which I translate here from French, clearly indicates a complicated outbreak of flu:

> On April 30th, twenty-three indigenous people showed up to the second appointment complaining of morbid symptoms that had appeared suddenly during the preceding hours, and which can be summed up like this: High temperatures of 38° to 40°, strong coughs sometimes leading to vomiting, headaches, back pain, widespread muscle pain . . . . On the first of May, during the morning visit, forty-three new cases of the same disease were observed in the same Unit . . . increasingly strong coughing, with blood coughed up, but which, under examination, seemed to be of pharyngeal origin, traces of bronchitis in both lungs, areas of congestion in the same organs.

23 ASSA, volume 814.

In addition to these two hypotheses that I have raised, there must also be other reasons why the excess mortality rates attributable to the Spanish flu pandemic were higher in most Mediterranean countries, such as Italy and Spain. Ansart et al. (2009) publish a rate of 15.1 deaths per 1,000 inhabitants in Italy; 12.0 per 1,000 inhabitants in Spain; and a figure for Portugal (which seems very high to me) of 22.3 deaths per 1,000 inhabitants—which Nunes et al. (2018) lower to 19.5 per 1,000 inhabitants. These figures contrast with the 7.3 deaths per 1,000 inhabitants in France; 7.7 per 1,000 in Switzerland; 6.6 per 1,000 in Germany; and 6.2 in the Netherlands.

## Forty Million Dead Worldwide

I started this book discussing the trivialization of the account of the Spanish flu pandemic and the falsehoods that have prevailed to this day. The account we historians give of the diseases, and the data and figures we publish, is not irrelevant; it is sometimes consulted and taken into account when making important decisions. For example, on July 21, 2020, the EU passed a 750-billion-euro economic plan, the allocation of which took into account the impact[24] of COVID-19 in each country.[25]

24 "L'Europe arrache un plan de 750 milliards," *Le Monde*, July 22, 2020.

25 "España recibirá 140.000 millones del fondo de recuperación, de los que 72.700 serán en subsidios," *El País*, July 21, 2020.

A lot of data about the 1918 flu pandemic has been manipulated. Some of it was manipulated from the start, at the end of the Great War, among other reasons because of the clash of strategic, political, and economic interests that culminated in the Treaty of Versailles. The most serious manipulation is the idea that one hundred million people died—which is why I want to give my own estimate for the number of dead caused by the Spanish flu pandemic worldwide. At that time, the population of the world was 1,825,000,000, distributed among the continents as follows in table 4.1.

Table 4.1. Population by continent in 1918 (1914).
Source: Dupâquier, 1998.

| | |
|---|---|
| Asia | 1,054,000,000 (57.8%) |
| Europe | 450,000,000 (24.7%) |
| America | 184,000,000 (10.1%) |
| Africa | 128,000,000 (7.0%) |
| Oceania | 8,000,000 (0.4%) |
| **Worldwide** | **1,825,000,000** |

The first estimate for pandemic deaths worldwide was made by Jordan (1927), who calculated that 21,542,283 people had died, or 12.0 dead per 1,000 inhabitants. Webster and Laver (1975) suggested that between 20 and 50 million had died; Schild (1977) stated between 15 and 50 million; and Beveridge (1978) proposed between

15 and 25 million. Only one voice stands apart substantially: Burnet (1979) estimated that there had been between 50 and 100 million victims. In recent years, two important articles in a medical history journal laid out geographical and global mortality. The first one, by Patterson and Pyle (1991), estimated the deceased at between 24,700,000 and 39,300,000. Two other investigators, Johnson and Mueller (2002), gave the figure of 48,798,038 deaths. Phillips and Killingray's collective book (2003) also provides global data and data for many countries around the world.

My own impression is that the number of deaths worldwide from the Spanish flu pandemic must have been around 40,000,000. The keys to this estimate are in China (400 million inhabitants) and India (320 million inhabitants). In the latter country, the British colonial authorities of the time estimated that 6 million had died as a result of the pandemic. More recently, Chandra, Kuljanin, and Wray (2012) and Chandra and Kassens-Noor (2014) have provided us with data on the geographical and temporal distribution of the pandemic, estimating the deceased at 13.8 million. China's data is unreliable; deaths are supposed to have been significant in 1917 but less so in 1918 (Langford 2005), with highly speculative numbers of between 4 and 10 million.

In the rest of Asia, including the Ottoman Empire, Persia, and Russia, the total population was below 300 million inhabitants. There is no reliable data on Russia, due to World War I, the revolution, and the civil war that followed. The flu pandemic was one more calamity that it suffered, and what was to become the Soviet Union lost millions of inhabitants in those years. From very fragmentary data from M. Azizi, Raees, and F. Azizi (2010), Yolun (2012), and others, the death figures could be between 5 and 10 million. In Africa and other parts of the world, there are no reliable administrative records, so their data are also speculative (I will take into account the 3% flu mortality rate for which we have records in port cities in West Africa, but there was probably not such a high rate of mortality in the interior).

Table 4.2. Estimate of deaths from the Spanish flu pandemic worldwide (A. Erkoreka)

| | **Population** | **Flu Mortality Rate** | **Estimated Flu Deaths** |
|---|---|---|---|
| Asia | 1,054,000,000 (57.8%) | 2–3% ? | 22,800,000–33,800,000 |
| Europe | 450,000,000 (24.7%) | 1% | 4,500,000 |
| America | 184,000,000 (10.1%) | 1% | 1,840,000 |
| Africa | 128,000,000 (7.0%) | 3% ? | 3,840,000 |
| Oceania | 8,000,000 (0.4%) | 1% | 800,000 |
| **Worldwide** | **1,825,000,000 (100%)** | **2.2%** | 33,780,000–44,780,000 (*circa* **40,000,000**) |

# Chapter 5
# COVID-19 in 2020

A century after the Spanish flu pandemic and half a century after the Hong Kong flu pandemic, in 2020 we saw the arrival of a new pandemic that has led to a real global cataclysm. Its medical, economic, demographic, political, and social consequences will be felt for many years.

## First Wave (Spring 2020)

### *Wuhan Coronavirus*

Wuhan is the capital of Hubei Province; it has eleven million inhabitants and is on the banks of the Blue River (Yangtse). It has historically been the natural crossing point over this great river and the crossroads in China for people going to the capital, Beijing (Bei-jing: "capital of the north"); Nanjing (Nan-jing: "capital of the south"); Dongjing ("capital of the east"), and, to the west, Xing ("capital of the west": Xi'an). It is also the midpoint of the railway between Beijing and Canton. Therefore, epidemiologically, it is a very important hub, well connected with the whole country, and a place from which a pandemic can easily spread over the whole territory. The city has an important biosafety level 4 (P4) laboratory and has grown at an unimaginable rate over recent years, causing irremediable ecological damage to flora and fauna in the surrounding environment, and, probably, the transfer of this zoonosis to humans, and its spread, like a wildfire, to people around the world.

The real causes of COVID-19 and the pandemics and epidemics of recent decades—and those to come—are the overpopulation, pollution, destruction of the environment, and climate change that we humans have been inflicting on the earth over recent years. AIDS, Ebola, some cases of avian influenza (H5N1, H7N9, H5N8), SARS, influenza A (H1N1), MERS, Zika, and chikungunya, among others, have begun to be a serious problem. In addition to those, new microorganisms are bound to appear in coming years, causing pandemics and crises similar to that of 2020. Disease historians have linked historical pandemics to zoonoses and environmental disorders. Examples are (as we remarked in Chapter 1) the sixth-century *pestis justinianea*; the so-called "Little Ice Age" at the time of the Black Death in the fourteenth century; the eruption of Tambora on the island of Sumbawa (Indonesia), which led to the first cholera pandemic of the nineteenth century; and the terrible First World War with its millions of soldiers and displaced workers from all over the world living in inhumane conditions, subjected to war gases and toxic substances, leading to the Spanish flu pandemic.

In autumn 2019, there was a coronavirus species-leap from a bat to a person through some other animal, and the virus began to be transmitted among humans immediately. Its first signs were detected in a fresh market, or "wet market," where live animals are sold for domestic consumption, in Wuhan. On the last day of the year, the new virus was provisionally given the name 2019-nCoV. On January 3, 2020, the Chinese authorities notified the World Health Organization (WHO-OMS) of an outbreak of pneumonia of unknown origin affecting forty-four patients, eleven of them severe. On the ninth of January, the first European media reported on the new disease, *Le Monde*'s headline being, "*Une pneumonie d'origine inconnue en Chine*," and stating that "officially, a hundred people have contracted a virus that could belong to the same family as SARS (Severe Acute Respiratory Syndrome)." On January 20, the WHO published its first *Situation Report*,[26] declaring 282 cases and 6 dead.

## Quarantine

*Quarantine* is a word and a concept that we had forgotten about, and that appears repeatedly with a symbolic figure—forty days—in different events in the Bible. We are interested in the account of the Flood, the forty days of rain to exterminate all living things on the earth, and the forty days with

26 World Health Organization, *Novel Coronavirus (2019-nCoV). Situation Report-1*, January 21, 2020, https://www.who.int/docs/default-source/coronaviruse/situation-reports/20200121-sitrep-1-2019-ncov.pdf?sfvrsn=20a99c10_4

the Ark stuck in the mud on Mount Ararat until life returned to the earth (Genesis, 6–9).

And that is the meaning the term *quarantine* took on once more in 2020: at two o'clock in the morning on January 23, the Chinese authorities reported the closure of Wuhan to prevent the spread of the disease. Confinement measures were to take effect at ten o'clock on the morning of that day, when 1,100 cases had already been diagnosed, and forty-one people had died. This first quarantine affected twenty million people, and New Year's festivities were cancelled to "efficiently stop the spread of the virus."[27]

The Chinese epidemiologist who made this decision was Zhong Nanshan, aged 83, who had managed the SARS pandemic that had emerged in China's Guangdong Province in November 2002. That pandemic, after infecting eight thousand people in twenty-nine countries and causing more than seven hundred deaths, had disappeared, SARS-CoV ceasing to spread in July 2003. This Chinese epidemiologist explained to Wuhan journalists that the only way to fight a disease for which there was no vaccine or specific treatment was early detection, early isolation, and social distancing[28]—in other words, the most primitive and effective methods.

27 "En Chine, trois villes en quarantaine et les festivités du Nouvel An annulées en raison du virus." *Le Monde*, January 23, 2020. ("Après Wuhan, épicentre du virus, Huanggang et Ezhou ont mis en place un confinement pour 'enrayer efficacement la propagation du virus.' ")

28 "El héroe que descubrió el SARS sigue las pistas del coronavirus en China," *El Comercio*, January 24, 2020.

In the fight against the new SARS-CoV-2 pandemic, the measures we have known and practiced since ancient times—isolation, confinement, health cordons, quarantines, and expurgation[29]—were once again imposed and applied in mass, with an intensity and geographical reach such as had never before been seen throughout history. During the spring of 2020, a large part of the planet's population was confined, and at times five billion people were in lockdown. Work in many sectors was halted; air, sea, and land communications were paralyzed; and the economy of a good part of the world froze, causing, by summer of 2020, a very serious economic and social crisis.

## Pandemic Spread

In February, the disease began to spread rapidly around the center of China and, in March, around Europe, the Middle East, America, and the rest of the world. The growth figures for the pandemic are exponential: on February 1, the WHO officially identified 14,380 cases and 304 dead worldwide; on March 1, 87,137 cases, 2,977 dead, and 58 affected countries. In mid-February, the new virus was definitively named SARS-CoV-2, recognizing its link to SARS-CoV, which had caused the 2002–2003

29 Joan March and Anton Erkoreka, "Combatiendo las pandemias desde hace tiempo. Nada nuevo bajo el sol. Aprendamos del pasado y no lo repitamos en el futuro," *elDiario.es*, April 4, 2020, https://www.eldiario.es/norte/vientodelnorte/coronavirus-salud_6_1013208680.html

pandemic. The disease that is produced by the new virus was named COVID-19.

In February, the avalanche of publications on the subject began, as did the first clinical reports on patients of the Chinese outbreak:[30] 44,672 laboratory-confirmed cases by PCR, of whom 2.3% died. Eighty percent of these patients were over the age of 60, many with previous pathologies that had worsened their prognosis—especially cardiovascular diseases (10%), diabetes (7%), chronic respiratory diseases (6%), etc.

On February 12, the WHO declared the disease "public enemy number one." In Europe it began sharply on February 21, with an intense outbreak of COVID-19 appearing in a small village in northern Italy, Codogno, which became the ground zero for Europe's pandemic. Immediately, the authorities isolated eleven towns and confined fifty thousand people. From there, massive confinements for the entire population became the norm, until reaching levels never seen in the history of medicine, between the months of March and May.

Despite the seriousness of the situation (Italy identified its first indigenous case on February 21, Spain on February 25, and France on February 29) and information coming from countries in the Far East and the Middle East, the authorities did not act diligently, delaying quarantine measures and

30 Zhonghua et al., "The epidemiological characteristics of an outbreak of 2019 novel coronavirus diseases (COVID-19) in China," *Chinese Center for Disease Control and Prevention,* February 10, 2020; 41(2): 145-151.

thus favoring the spread of the virus. In Spain, the left-wing government promoted the mass demonstrations held on Women's Day (March 8); in France, the first round of municipal elections was held; and soccer matches and other mass events were held in all three countries. Spain declared a "State of Emergency" on March 14, confining the entire population to their homes until June 20, at which time the restriction ended after several phases of de-escalation. States took the reins of the situation, relegating autonomous regions to a second level. In Euskadi (the Basque Country), the Basque government made its "Health Emergency Declaration" on March 13, although some of us moved faster than that, seeing that the pandemic was well advanced, and closed our Basque Museum of the History of Medicine on March 9. The University of the Basque Country closed some centers, such as the Aulas de la Experiencia, earlier, in the middle of that week.

At that time, on March 12, the WHO reported 125,048 cases and 4,613 deaths worldwide; 7,660 cases and 1,266 deaths in Italy; in Spain, 4,200 cases and 120 deaths; and in France, 3,661 cases and 79 deaths. On April 1, Spain reached 100,000 cases and 9,000 dead; Araba, Bizkaia, and Gipuzkoa had around 15,000 cases and 250 dead.

As of mid-April, the official rates estimated by Johns Hopkins University were, for Spain, 397.9 cases per 100,000 inhabitants and 40 dead per 100,000 inhabitants; for Italy, 273.2 cases and 35.8 dead per 100,000 inhabitants; for France, 161.2

cases and 16.2 dead per 100,000 inhabitants; for the USA, 192.2 cases and 8.6 deaths per 100,000 inhabitants; for China, 5.8 cases and 0.2 deaths per 100,000 inhabitants; for Chile, 43.3 cases and 0.5 dead per 100,000 inhabitants; and for Australia, 25.3 cases and 0.2 dead per 100,000 inhabitants.

The WHO's *Situation Report* (132) of May 31, 2020, gave the official, accurate figure of 5,934,936 cases and 367,166 deaths worldwide. In Europe, there were totals of 2,142,547 cases and 180,085 deaths. Spain's figures were 239,600 cases and 29,043 deaths from COVID-19. France had 148,436 cases and 28,717 deaths (see fig. 5.1).

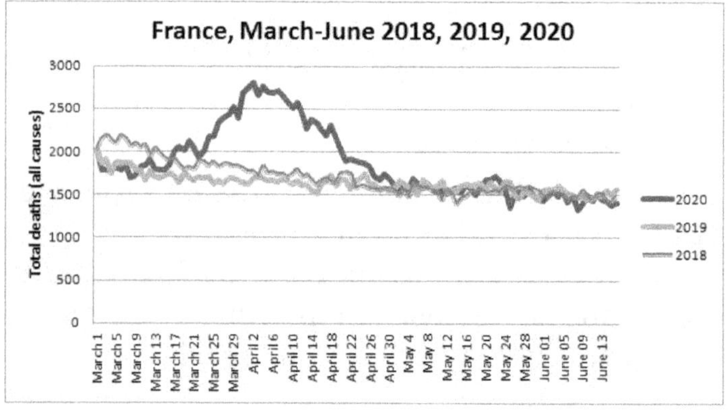


Figure 5.1. Excess mortality in France attributable to the coronavirus pandemic, compared to mortality in 2018 and 2019. Source: *Insee.*

At the end of June, Europe's first wave ended, and the phase of de-escalating began, with people trying to return to normal, or, as it was called in the media, "new normality." With the beginning of summer and the return of people to the streets, beaches, and so on, and with some people not even taking minimum precautions to avoid the spread of the virus (social distancing, masks, etc.), the disease began to reappear in different places around Spain and, by mid-July, there were two hundred epidemic outbreaks, and by the end of August, one thousand. And where the pandemic had begun, in China, there were major new outbreaks in places such as Beijing, and in neighboring Korea. In America and Africa, the pandemic was still in the growth phase. By the end of June 2020, there had been 10 million officially confirmed cases and 500,000 deaths from coronavirus worldwide. The United States accounted for a quarter of these official figures, with 2.5 million confirmed cases and 125,000 deaths.

The July 18 *Situation Report*[31] gave official figures of 13,876,441 cases of COVID-19 and 593,087 deaths worldwide. The Americas were at the top of the table, with 7,306,371 cases and 302,508 deaths. Johns Hopkins University data, often followed by the media around the world,[32] reported 14,301,124 cases and 602,315 deaths from COVID-19 on that day. Data discrepancies, depending on the different

31 https://www.who.int/docs/default-source/coronaviruse/situation-reports/20200718-covid-19-sitrep-180.pdf?sfvrsn=39b31718_2

32 https://coronavirus.jhu.edu/map.html

sources consulted, were the norm. The differences by country and continent were also very large. We are going to examine the death rates per 1,000,000 inhabitants provided by Johns Hopkins University in mid-July: Spain, 608.1; Italy, 579.4; France, 450.1; Portugal, 163.2; Belgium, 857.5; United Kingdom, 679.8; Sweden (which had not carried out quarantine policies during this first wave), 549.2; its neighbor Norway, which had imposed measures and closed their shared border, 47.7; Israel, 43.2; Iran, 166.3; USA, 422.8; Mexico, 297.7; Brazil, 366.1; and in the southern hemisphere, at the beginning of its winter—Chile, 389.2; Argentina, 47.4; South Africa, 80.8; and Australia (with the lowest rate), 4.6 dead per 1 million inhabitants. As is clear from this data, the first wave of COVID-19 severely affected the Northern Hemisphere, where it was winter and spring, but also, in a milder way, the southern hemisphere, during its summer and autumn. This was a major difference compared with seasonal flus, which jump from one hemisphere to another following winter.

## One Dead per 1,000 Inhabitants of Spain in First Wave

In France, the number of confirmed cases at the end of June 2020 was 163,000, with 30,000 dead. In Spain, by that time, official cases had risen to 250,000, and the number of officially recognized deaths was approaching 30,000, although the figures of excess mortality almost doubled that figure. Comparing the official data with excess mortality in Spain,[33] between March 14 and May 25, 2020, there are substantial discrepancies. Officially, 28,109 people had died, but according to MoMo (*Sistema de Monitorización de la Mortalidad Diaria*, Daily Mortality Monitoring System) the figure was 43,002; according to the Spanish Association of Funeral Services Professionals, AESPROF, 43,985; and in INE's figures (National Statistics Institute), 47,123. In other words, the official mortality rate of 0.5 per 1,000 inhabitants doubles when the calculation is based on excess mortality, giving us a figure of 1.0 deaths per 1,000 inhabitants in Spain—which, in my opinion, is the real number of deaths in the country during the first wave of the coronavirus pandemic.

In Navarre, with a population of 660,887 (2020), taking data from June 1, 498 people officially died and, based on excess mortality of 658, the mortality rate was somewhere between 0.7 and 0.9 per 1,000 inhabitants. In the Basque Autonomous Community, with a population of 2,188,017 (2019), 1,454 people officially died from coronavirus (according to excess mortality, 1,636), so the mortality rate was between 0.6 and 0.7 per 1,000 inhabitants.

33 Anton Erkoreka and Josu Hernando, "Ha fallecido 1 de cada 1.000 habitantes en España a causa de la pandemia," *eldiario.es*, June 8, 2020, https://www.eldiario.es/norte/vientodelnorte/fallecido-habitantes-Espana-causa-COVID-19_6_1035956409.html

A significant fact is that 240,195 people were analyzed in Araba, Bizkaia, and Gipuzkoa on June 28—using PCR plus rapid tests on single people—with 20,926 testing positive (61% women; 38.9% men; 0.1% unregistered). According to official data from the Basque Health Service, Osakidetza, 1,611 people had died from COVID-19. (Age distribution is shown in figure 5.2.) By gender, from the age of 70, men are more likely to die than women from COVID-19, since, at those advanced ages, the number of men alive is much lower than that of women. And despite this huge difference in the absolute number of men and women, according to MoMo men made up 50.7% of excess mortality, while women accounted for 49.3%.

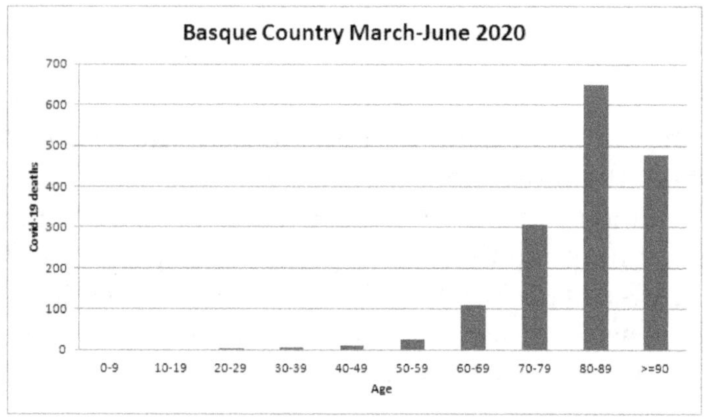


Figure 5.2. Age of the deceased during the first wave of COVID-19 in Araba, Bizkaia, and Gipuzkoa. Source: *Osakidetza*.

This concentration of deaths in the most advanced age groups has been seen in COVID-19 statistics published all around the world. In absolute numbers, there is a maximum concentration in men over 80, and that decreases as age goes down.

The deaths of most elderly men and women as a result of COVID-19 took place in care homes. Attention to this segment of the population has been poor and lacking in transparency, which shows clear failures in assistance to the elderly, its privatization, and the low level of quality of care. According to *El País*,[34] "Eighty-six percent of the nearly 30,000 officially recognized dead in Spain were over 70 years old. Of these, the highest percentage were over 80. And there could be many more if we examine data about this year's excess deaths compared with data from the year before published by the National Statistical Institute."

Some health services—for example in the Community of Madrid, Castilla-La Mancha, and in Castilla y León—were overwhelmed, without any room in their ICUs, having to organize field hospitals in open-air venues (such as IFEMA, a convention center in Madrid) or next to the hospitals, and were unable to properly care for the entire population.

34 Pablo de Llano, "Así perdimos a la generación que cambió España," *El País*, June 27, 2020.

## Some Parallels and Lessons: 1918 Flu and 2020 CoV

Throughout the book I pointed out that the first wave of COVID-19 has significant similarities with the first wave of Spanish flu. Both SARS-CoV-2 and H1N1 appeared suddenly as a result of mutations that took them from an animal (bat, pangolin, bird, pig, for example) to people and, at a later stage, to massive contagion from person to person. As in other pandemics, the country of origin of COVID-19 was China, which may also have been the origin of Spanish flu. But the lack of information and lack of transparency in the communist regime that governs that country delayed coronavirus containment measures during its initial outbreak in late 2019. Both coronavirus and flu viruses have an extreme capacity to spread, rapidly around the world and reaching the most improbable places. Its transmission route is from person to person by air. SARS-CoV-2 and H1N1 are of unusual virulence and cause very serious clinical cases with complications of respiratory and other organs and systems, such as cardiovascular, CNS, kidneys, etc. In Spanish flu, these facets were not well studied. After the first wave of COVID-19 we got to know them better, although there are still many unknowns.

Both the 1918 and the 2020 pandemics, in addition to their mortality and morbidity, have had serious health, economic, demographic, and political impact on social relations, customs, and all aspects of life.

I have already stated that the excess mortality rate of the first wave of Spanish flu in Madrid, in May–June 1918, was between 1 death per 1,000 inhabitants (Chowell et al. 2014) and 1.7 deaths per 1,000 inhabitants (A. Erkoreka 2017). One hundred years later, despite advances in medical science, we found that during the first wave of COVID-19, in the spring of 2020, the excess mortality rate attributable to the pandemic in Madrid was 1.3 dead per 1,000 inhabitants (according to the official figures) or, using the actual mortality figures we have mentioned—as provided by MoMo, AESPROF, and INE—a maximum, real rate of 2.3 deaths per 1,000 in Madrid.

By the end of July, the Spanish government had recognized only 28,441 deaths from COVID-19 across the state. Considering that the population of Spain is 47,649,000 (2020), the officially recognized mortality rate was 0.6 deaths per 1,000 inhabitants. But, using the excess mortality figures (ranging from 43,002 deaths recorded by MoMo to the 47,123 stated by INE), during the first wave of COVID-19, the excess mortality rate can be set at around 1 deceased per 1,000 inhabitants for the whole of Spain.

The reflection that we can make in the summer of 2020 is that, after one hundred years, a new virus which broke out in China and expanded rapidly around the world caused, in its first wave, a mortality rate of 1 per 1,000 inhabitants. That is exactly the same mortality rate that the new H1N1 virus caused after appearing in the spring of 1918; it, too, spread rapidly all over the world. Despite the obvious advances in medicine in this century, and using all our resources, we failed to reduce mortality or improve on 1918 rates.

Some patterns in data were also repeated in different regions of Spain during the two pandemics. The community of Madrid (6,663,394 inhabitants in 2019), as I have already stated, had, on June 1, an official, minimum mortality rate of 1.3 deaths per 1,000 inhabitants, and a maximum, real rate of 2.3 per 1,000 inhabitants. At the opposite end are the Canary Islands (2,220,270 inhabitants in 2019), with a rate of 0.04 deaths per 1,000 inhabitants. The same happened in 1918 during the first wave in Madrid, and during all waves in the Canary Islands (which were not affected by Spanish flu). We do not fully understand the reasons for these parallels between the pandemics of 1918 and 2020, but we have seen that one hundred years ago, like now, Madrid and the Canary Islands were at opposite ends of the statistics during the first wave. This is a very important fact, and we should examine the geographical, climatic, urban, social, and human reasons that made Madrid the most affected region during the first wave of 1918, and once more in 2020.

Just as we have detected this extreme difference between the center of the Iberian Peninsula and those fortunate islands in the middle of the Atlantic, we have also seen a difference in both pandemics between the Mediterranean countries (Italy and Spain—greatly affected by both pandemics) and the Nordic countries (with lower morbidity and mortality rates).

As for the Basque Country, the first wave of Spanish flu in 1918 caused a mortality rate of 0.6 per 1,000 inhabitants in Bilbao. COVID-19, in the spring of 2020, caused a similar mortality rate of between 0.6 and 0.7 deaths per 1,000 inhabitants in the three provinces of the Basque Autonomous Community, as calculated by official data about deaths and excess mortality (see fig. 5.3). In Navarre, the mortality rate attributable to the pandemic ranges from 0.7 to 0.9 per 1,000 inhabitants. As stated earlier, the fact that we are facing the same rate in 2020 as in the spring of 1918, despite the advances in medicine over the intervening century, is very worrying.

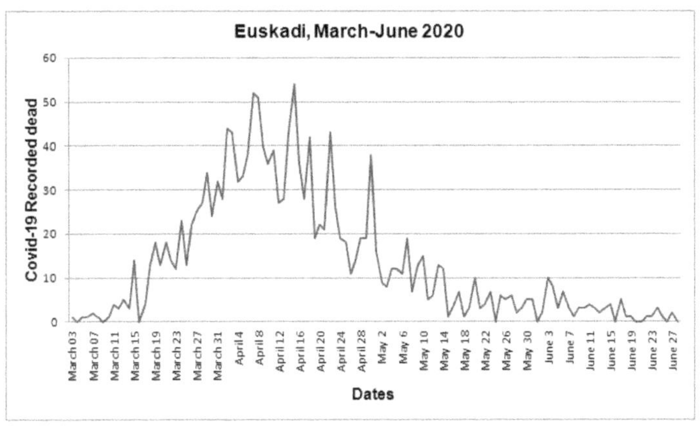


Figure 5.3. Daily deaths from COVID-19 in the Basque Autonomous Community between March and May 2020. Source: *Osakidetza*.

I conclude with the reflection that we must be humble and recognize that scientists do not know or master everything. There are always questions, incomprehensible facts, and unanswered questions regarding the patterns of all pandemics, whether COVID-19, Spanish flu, or any other pandemic that may appear in future years in the heart of Asia or Africa, and that will reach us in Europe or America. We must be prepared—*Gird your loins and light your lamps* (Luke 12:35)—to deal promptly with new pandemics that appear.

# Bibliography

## Primary Sources (Manuscripts and Archival Sources)

In recent years, I have consulted and collected first-hand information and materials in the main archives in Western European capitals. In Paris, I consulted the *Archives du services de santé des armées* (ASSA) at Val-de-Grâce (Paris), where its typed catalogue was of great help (Fabre 1977). I also consulted the *Archives de Paris* and the *Bibliotheque interuniversitaire de médecine* (BIUM). In Rome, I examined the *Archivio Storico Capitalino,* and the *Biblioteca Universitaria Alessandrina* at the *Universitá degli Studi di Roma La Sapienza.* In the Vatican City, the *Archivio Segreto Vaticano.* In Madrid, I examined the *Archivo General de la Villa de Madrid* and the *Hemeroteca Municipal de Madrid,* both in Conde Duque Arts Centre. In Toledo, the Army Museum archives. Other archives in smaller cities, such as Porto, Pau, Biarritz, and Bilbao (*Archivo Municipal de Bilbao*), have helped me to compare data. In the Basque Country, with the help of medical students at the University of the Basque Country (UPV/EHU) and some other independent researchers, we have been able to examine several parish archives in Bizkaia,

Gipuzkoa, Navarre, and Araba. We have also consulted personally, and in collaboration, some civil archives in the Northern Basque Country, Vitoria-Gasteiz, and Bilbao.

## Printed Primary Sources (Official Documents, Reports, and Newspapers)

The second set of main sources used were yearbooks and newsletters published by public institutions, which provide official statistical data, along with the advantages and disadvantages of managing these sources. We must mention among others: *Annuaire statistique de la ville de Paris, Bollettino di Statistica del Comune di Roma, Bollettino dell'Ufficio Municipale del Lavoro, Estadística Demográfica Madrid, Boletín de la Estadística Municipal de Madrid*, and *Boletín Mensual de Estadística Sanitaria de Bilbao*. These publications, some of which are incomplete, have been supplemented using archival records as well as newspapers, magazines, and books. Regarding the quality of this data, it must be said that, at the beginning of the twentieth century, French and German medicine were the most advanced in the world, so the clinical and epidemiological data collected from newsletters and medical reports is highly reliable. With regard to registration problems and military censorship in France, it should be remembered that World War I ended in November 1918, and that a lot of data, such as Parisian statistics from 1915 to 1918, was published three years later, in 1921.

## Printed Secondary Sources

The third and highest-quality sources of information, because of all the filters they go through, are papers published in biomedicine journals, mainly on the pandemics and epidemics over recent decades. In this case, my guide has been PubMed, which is the medical database of the Library of Congress of the United States, which has registered 170 million items (24.8 million books, 15 million articles in print collections, and 130 million in unclassified collections). The "influenza" entry has 134,445 quotations; "1918 pandemic influenza" gets 1,131 results; "coronavirus," 39,065; and "COVID-19," 35,054 (see July 25, 2020). On January 1, 2020, when the pandemic had not yet begun, there were only 844 references to "coronavirus," which gives an idea of the avalanche of publications on the subject since then.

Ansart, Séverine, Camille Pelat, Pierre - Yves Boelle, Fabrice Carrat, Antoine Flahault, and Alain - Jacques Valleron. "Mortality burden of the 1918–1919 influenza pandemic in Europe." Influenza and other respiratory viruses 3, no. 3 (2009): 99-106.

Azizi, Mohammad Hossein, Jalali Gh A. Raeis, and Farzaneh Azizi. "A History of the 1918 Spanish Influenza Pandemic and its Impact on Iran." Arch Iran Med 13 (2010): 262-265.

Barry, John M. The Great Influenza. The Story of the Deadliest Pandemic in History. New York: Penguin Books, 2005.

Berche, Patrick. Faut-il encore avoir peur de la grippe? Histoire des pandémies. Paris: Odile Jacob, 2012.

Bertillon, Jacques. La grippe a Paris et dans quelques autres villes de France et de l'étranger en 1889–1890. Paris: Imprimerie Municipale, 1892.

Beveridge, W. I. B. Influenza: The Last Great Plague. An Unfinished Story of Discovery. New York: Prodist, 1978.

Bilbao, City Hall. Memoria de la organización y funcionamiento de los servicios municipales para combatir la epidemia grippal. Año de 1918. (Memory of the organization and operation of municipal services to combat the influenza epidemic. Year 1918.) Bilbao: Imp Lerchundi, 1919.

Bouhdiba, Sofiane. Pavillon jaune: Historie de la quarantaine, de la Peste à Ebola. Paris: L'Harmattan, 2016.

Burnet, F. M. "Portraits of Viruses: Influenza Virus A." Intervirology 11, no. 4 (1979): 201-214.

Chandra, Siddharth, and Eva Kassens-Noor. "The Evolution of Pandemic Influenza: Evidence from India, 1918–19." BMC Infectious Diseases 14, no. 1 (2014): 510.

Chandra, Siddharth, Goran Kuljanin, and Jennifer Wray. "Mortality from the Influenza Pandemic of 1918–1919: The Case of India." Demography 49, no. 3 (2012): 857-865.

Chowell, Gerardo, Anton Erkoreka, Cécile Viboud, and Beatriz Echeverri-Dávila. "Spatial-Temporal Excess Mortality Patterns of the 1918–1919 Influenza Pandemic in Spain." BMC Infectious Diseases 14, no. 1 (2014): 371.

Collins, Selwyn D. "Age and Sex Incidence of Influenza and Pneumonia Morbidity and Mortality in the Epidemic of 1928–29 with Comparative Data for the Epidemic of 1918–19." Public Health Reports (1896-1970) 33 (1931): 1909-1937.

Crosby, Alfred W. America's Forgotten Pandemic. The Influenza of 1918. 2nd ed. Cambridge: Cambridge University Press, 2003.

Cui, Jie, Fang Li, and Zheng-Li Shi. "Origin and Evolution of Pathogenic Coronaviruses." Nature Reviews Microbiology 17, no. 3 (2019): 181-192.

Darmon, Pierre. "Une tragédie dans la tragédie: la grippe espagnole en France (avril 1918–avril 1919)." Annales de Démographie Historique, no. 2 (2000): 153-175.

Davis, Ryan A. The Spanish Flu. Narrative and Cultural Identity in Spain, 1918. New York: Palgrave Macmillan, 2013.

Dupâquier, J., introduction to Histoire des populations de l'Europe. II. La révolution démographique. 1750-1914, by Jean-Pierre Bardet and Jacques Dupâquier, 7-17. Paris: Fayard, 1998.

Echeverri Dávila, Beatriz. La gripe española. La pandemia de 1918-1919. Madrid: CIS-Siglo XXI, 1993.

Erkoreka, Anton, ed. "La pandemia de gripe española (1918-1920) desde el País Vasco / The Spanish influenza pandemic (1918-1920) from the Basque Country." Gaceta Médica de Bilbao 118 (Supl 1) (2021): S1-S97.

Erkoreka, Anton. "Safe Village During the 1918–1919 Influenza Pandemic in Spain and Portugal." Journal of Preventive Medicine and Hygiene 61 (2020): E137-E142.

Erkoreka, Anton. "Y se le llamó gripe española". Investigación y Ciencia, 489 (junio 2017): 52-53.

http://www.investigacionyciencia.es/revistas/investigacion-y-ciencia/un-xito-en-la-lucha-contra-el-alzhimer-706/y-se-le-llam-gripe-espaola-15313

Erkoreka, Anton. "The Spanish Influenza Pandemic in Occidental Europe (1918–1920) and Victim Age." Influenza and Other Respiratory Viruses 4, no. 2 (2010): 81-89.

Erkoreka, Anton. 2009a. "Origins of the Spanish Influenza Pandemic (1918–1920) and its Relation to the First World War." Journal of Molecular and Genetic Medicine 3, no. 2 (2009): 190-194.

Erkoreka, Anton. 2009b. "La pandémie de grippe espagnole sur la côte basque (1918–1919)." Bulletin du Musée basque 173 (2009): 83-90.

http://www.ehu.es/documents/1970815/2421082/2009+Erkoreka.+Pand%C3%A9mie+1918+C%C3%B4te+Basque

Erkoreka, Anton. 2008a. "Epidémies en Pays basque: de la peste noire à la grippe espagnole." Histoire des sciences médicales 42 (2008): 113-122.

Erkoreka, Anton. 2008b. "Spanish Influenza in the Heart of Europe. A Study of a Significant Sample of the Basque Population." Gesnerus 65 (2008): 30-41.

Erkoreka, Anton. La pandemia de gripe española en el País Vasco (1918-1919). Bilbao: MHM, 2006. http://www.ehu.es/documents/1970815/0/Pandemia_de_gripe_espa%C3%B1ola

Erkoreka, Mikel. "Economía y salud pública en el País Vasco en tiempos de la gripe española." Gaceta Médica de Bilbao 118, no. S1 (2021): 55-62.

Erkoreka, Mikel, Josu Hernando, Anton Erkoreka, and Eduardo Alonso. "Impacto económico, demográfico y social de la pandemia de gripe española en Bizkaia (1918-1920)." Investigaciones de Historia Económica 17 (2021): 42-53.

Fabre, A. Archives historiques du service de santé militaires conservées au Musée du Val de Grace. Paris: Catalogue dactylographiée, 3 vol. circa 1977.

Febvre, Lucien. Combats pour l'histoire. Paris: Armand Collin, 1952.

Febvre, Lucien. Pour une histoire à part entire. Paris: SEVPEN, 1962.

Frémeaux, Jacques. Les colonies dans la Grand Guerre. Combats et épreuves des peuples d'Outre-mer. Cahors: 14-18 éditions, 2006.

Gagnon, Alain, Matthew S. Miller, Stacey A. Hallman, Robert Bourbeau, D. Ann Herring, David JD Earn, and Joaquín Madrenas. "Age-Specific Mortality During the 1918 Influenza

Pandemic: Unravelling the Mystery of High Young Adult Mortality." PloS One 8, no. 8 (2013): e69586.

Gomez, Gumersindo. Cómo se vive y cómo se muere en Bilbao. Reseña demográfica de la Villa de Bilbao. Bilbao, 1896.

Gondra, Juan, and Anton Erkoreka. "El Cuerpo Médico Municipal (1897-1937) y la pandemia de gripe española en Bilbao (1918-1920)." Bidebarrieta 21 (2010): 139-152.

Gozlan, Marc. "Il était une foi les coronavirus." Réalités Biomédicales 27 (mars 2020).

Grégoire de Tours. L'histoire des rois francs. Paris: Gallimard, 2012.

Gripe izurri-gexoa galazoteko Bilbao'ko Osalari-Bazkunak aginduten dauzan egin-bearrak = Instrucciones profilácticas aconsejadas por la Academia de Ciencias Médicas de Bilbao para combatir la epidemia gripal. Bilbao: Bizkaia-aldundijaren irarrkolea, 1918. In Erkoreka, Anton, La pandemia de gripe española en el País Vasco... 2006: 81-94. http://www.ehu.es/documents/1970815/0/Pandemia_de_gripe_espa%C3%B1ola

Hernando-Pérez, Josu. "La gripe española en Bilbao. Análisis demográfico de la pandemia y sus consecuencias desde diferentes fuentes de información." Gaceta Médica de Bilbao 118, no. S1 (2021): 19-26.

Jimeno Jurio, Jose María. "El año de la gripe." Punto y Hora de Euskal Herria 52 (1977): 26-30. Also in Obras Completas (Ed. D. Mariezkurrena), t. 13, Navarra 1917-1919. Reivindicaciones autonómicas. Pamplona-Iruña: Pamiela, 2006.

Johnson, Niall PAS. "The overshadowed killer: influenza in Britain in 1918-19," in The Spanish Influenza Pandemic of 1918-1919, by Howard Phillips and David Killingray, 132-155. London: Routledge, 2003.

Johnson, Niall PAS, and Juergen Mueller. "Updating the Accounts: Global Mortality of the 1918-1920 'Spanish' Influenza Pandemic." Bulletin of the History of Medicine 76 (2002): 105-115.

Jordan, Edwin O. Epidemic Influenza: A Survey. Chicago: American Medical Association, 1927.

Jorge, Ricardo. A influenza. Nova incursão peninsular. Relatório apresentado ao Conselho Superior de Higiene na sessão de 18 de Junho de 1918. Lisbon: Imprenta Nacional, 1918.

Langford, Christopher. "Did the 1918–19 Influenza Pandemic Originate in China?" Population and Development Review 31, no. 3 (2005): 473-505.

Le Roy Ladurie, Emmanuel. Historia humana y comparada del clima. Mexico: Fondo de Cultura Económica, 2017.

Ma, Li. La Chine et la Grande Guerre. Paris: CNRS Editions, 2019.

Madarieta-Revilla, Begoña. "La pandemia de gripe de 1918 en la población infantil de Bilbao." Gaceta Médica de Bilbao 118, no. S1 (2021): 35-40.

March, Joan, and Anton Erkoreka. "Aspectos históricos de los coronavirus que afectan a humanos." Medicina Balear 35, no. 4 (2020): 13-17.

Monteano, PJ. La ira de Dios. Los navarros en la era de la peste (1348-1723). Pamplona-Iruña: Pamiela, 2002.

Morens, David M., Jeffery K. Taubenberger, and Anthony S. Fauci. "The Persistent Legacy of the 1918 Influenza Virus." New England Journal of Medicine 361, no. 3 (2009): 225-229.

Morrow, John H. The Great War. An Imperial History. London: Routledge, 2004. Spanish edition: La Gran Guerra (2008).

Navarro García, Ramón. Análisis de la sanidad en España a lo largo del siglo XX. Madrid: Instituto de Salud Carlos III, 2002.

Nelson, Martha I., Cecile Viboud, Lone Simonsen, Ryan T. Bennett, Sara B. Griesemer, Kirsten St George, Jill Taylor, et al. "Multiple Reassortment Events in the Evolutionary History of H1N1 Influenza A Virus Since 1918." PLoS Pathogens 4, no. 2 (2008): 1-12.

Nunes, Baltazar, Susana Silva, Ana Rodrigues, Rita Roquette, Inês Batista, and Helena Rebelo-de-Andrade. "The 1918–1919 Influenza Pandemic in Portugal: A Regional Analysis of Death Impact." American Journal of Epidemiology 187, no. 12 (2018): 2541-2549.

Olson, Donald R., Lone Simonsen, Paul J. Edelson, and Stephen S. Morse. "Epidemiological Evidence of an Early Wave of the 1918 Influenza Pandemic in New York City." Proceedings of the National Academy of Sciences 102, no. 31 (2005): 11059-11063.

Oxford, John S., Rob Lambkin, Armine Sefton, R. Daniels, A. Elliot, R. Brown, and D. Gill. "A Hypothesis: The Conjunction of Soldiers, Gas, Pigs, Ducks, Geese and Horses in Northern France During the Great War Provided the Conditions for the Emergence of the 'Spanish' Influenza Pandemic of 1918–1919." Vaccine 23, no. 7 (2005): 940-945.

Oxford, John S., Armine Sefton, Richard Jackson, William Innes, Rod S. Daniels, and Niall PAS Johnson. "World War I may have Allowed the Emergence of 'Spanish' Influenza." The Lancet Infectious Diseases 2, no. 2 (2002): 111-114.

Patterson, K. David. Pandemic Influenza, 1700-1900: A Study in Historical Epidemiology. Totowa, N.J.: Rowman & Littlefield, 1986.

Patterson, K. David, and Gerald F. Pyle. "The Geography and Mortality of the 1918 Influenza Pandemic." Bulletin of the History of Medicine 65, no. 1 (1991): 4-21.

Phillips, Howard. "The Recent Wave of 'Spanish' Flu Historiography." Social History of Medicine 27, no. 4 (2014): 789-808.

Phillips, Howard, and David Killingray, eds. The Spanish Influenza Pandemic of 1918-1919. New Perspectives. London: Routledge, 2003.

Piga, A., and L. Lamas. Infecciones de tipo gripal. Madrid: Editorial Plus-Ultra, 1919.

Porras Gallo, María Isabel. Un reto para la sociedad madrileña: La epidemia de gripe de 1918-19. Madrid: Editorial Complutense, 1997.

Proust, A., et al. "Sur l'enquéte concernant l'épidémie de grippe de 1889–1890 en France." Bulletin de l'Académie de médecine 15 (1892): 510-531 and 16 (1892): 552-596.

Ramos Martínez, Jesús. "La pandemia de gripe de 1918 en Pamplona." Príncipe de Viana (Anexo 16) 53 (1992): 109-130.

Saillant, M. Tableau historique et raisonné des épidémies catharrales, vulgairement dites la grippe. Paris: Desaint, 1780.

Schild, G. G. "Influenza," in A Word Geography of Human Diseases, by Howe, G. Melvyn (ed.), 366. London-New York: Academic Press, 1977.

Schuck-Paim, Cynthia, G. Dennis Shanks, Francisco E. Almeida, and Wladimir J. Alonso. "Exceptionally High Mortality Rate of the 1918 Influenza Pandemic in the Brazilian Naval Fleet." Influenza and Other Respiratory Viruses 7, no. 1 (2013): 27-34.

Shanks, G. Dennis, Nick Wilson, Rebecca Kippen, and John F. Brundage. "The Unusually Diverse Mortality Patterns in the Pacific Region During the 1918–21 Influenza Pandemic: Reflections at the Pandemic's Centenary." The Lancet Infectious Diseases 18, no. 10 (2018). e323-e332.

Simonsen, Lone, Matthew J. Clarke, Lawrence B. Schonberger, Nancy H. Arden, Nancy J. Cox, and Keiji Fukuda. "Pandemic versus Epidemic Influenza Mortality: A Pattern of Changing Age Distribution." Journal of Infectious Diseases 178, no. 1 (1998): 53-60.

Smith, Gavin JD, Justin Bahl, Dhanasekaran Vijaykrishna, Jinxia Zhang, Leo LM Poon, Honglin Chen, Robert G. Webster, JS Malik Peiris, and Yi Guan. "Dating the Emergence of Pandemic Influenza Viruses." Proceedings of the National Academy of Sciences 106, no. 28 (2009): 11709-11712.

Spinney, Laura. El jinete pálido. 1918: La epidemia que cambió el mundo. Barcelona: Crítica, 2018.

Sydenham, Thomas. Opera Medica. Geneva: Fratres de Tournes, 1769.

Taubenberger, Jeffery K., and David M. Morens. "1918 Influenza: The Mother of All Pandemics." Emerging Infectious Diseases 12, no. 1 (2006): 15-22.

Taubenberger, Jeffery K., Ann H. Reid, Amy E. Krafft, Karen E. Bijwaard, and Thomas G. Fanning. "Initial Genetic Characterization of the 1918 'Spanish' Influenza Virus." Science 275, no. 5307 (1997): 1793-1796.

Taubenberger, Jeffery K., Ann H. Reid, Raina M. Lourens, Ruixue Wang, Guozhong Jin, and Thomas G. Fanning. "Characterization of the 1918 Influenza Virus Polymerase Genes." Nature 437, no. 7060 (2005): 889-893.

Tognotti, Eugenia. La 'Spagnola' in Italia. Storia dell'influenza che fece temere la fine del mondo (1918-19). Milano: Franco Angeli, 2002.

Tumpey, Terrence M., Christopher F. Basler, Patricia V. Aguilar, Hui Zeng, Alicia Solórzano, David E. Swayne, Nancy J. Cox, et al. "Characterization of the Reconstructed 1918 Spanish Influenza Pandemic Virus." Science 310, no. 5745 (2005): 77-80.

Uriarte, Antón. Historia del clima de la tierra. Vitoria-Gasteiz: Eusko Jaurlaritza, 2009.

Valleron, Alain-Jacques, Anne Cori, Sophie Valtat, Sofia Meurisse, Fabrice Carrat, and Pierre-Yves Boëlle. "Transmissibility and Geographic Spread of the 1889 Influenza Pandemic." Proceedings of the National Academy of Sciences 107, no. 19 (2010): 8778-8781.

Van Ho, Mireille L. Des vietnamiens dans la Grande Guerre. 50,000 recrues dans les usines françaises. Paris: Vendémiaire, 2014.

Viboud, Cécile, Jana Eisenstein, Ann H. Reid, Thomas A. Janczewski, David M. Morens, and Jeffery K. Taubenberger. "Age- and Sex-Specific Mortality Associated With the 1918–1919 Influenza Pandemic in Kentucky." The Journal of Infectious Diseases 207, no. 5 (2013): 721-729.

Viboud, Cécile, Theresa Tam, Douglas Fleming, Mark A. Miller, and Lone Simonsen. "1951 Influenza Epidemic, England and Wales, Canada, and the United States." Emerging Infectious Diseases 12, no. 4 (2006): 661-668.

Webster, R.G., and W.G. Laver. "Pandemic Variation of Influenza Viruses," in The Influenza Viruses and Influenza, by Edwin D. Kilbourne (ed.), 269-314. New York: Academic Press, 1975.

Wrigley, E.A., and R.S. Schofield. The Population History of England, 1541-1871. Cambridge: Cambridge University Press, 1989.

Yolun, Murat. "Íspanyol gribinin dünya ve Osmanli Devleti üzerindeki etkileri = The Impact of Spanish Influenza on the World and the Ottoman State." Master's thesis, Adiyaman Üniversitesi (Turkey), 2012

Zylberman, P. "A Holocaust in a Holocaust. The Great War and the 1918 Spanish Influenza Epidemic in France," in The Spanish Influenza Pandemic of 1918-19, by Howard Phillips and David Killingray, 191-201. London: Routledge, 2003.

www.ingramcontent.com/pod-product-compliance
Lightning Source LLC
LaVergne TN
LVHW010101110826
845155LV00028B/435

* 9 7 8 1 9 4 9 8 0 5 5 6 7 *